GOOD HUNTING.

DAYS WITH THE GOLDEN EAGLE

SETON GORDON
IN COLLABORATION WITH HIS WIFE
[AUDREY GORDON]

Whittles Publishing

vi

Typeset by
Whittles Publishing Services

Published by
Whittles Publishing Limited,
Roseleigh House,
Latheronwheel,
Caithness, KW5 6DW,
Scotland, UK
www.whittlespublishing.com

ISBN 1-870325-35-4

Printed by Bell & Bain Ltd., Glasgow

I have lived in eagle country most of my life, and in this book have endeavoured to give information of the golden eagle which has not appeared in print before

A great number of correspondents have helped me with much valuable information, and to them all I would tender my grateful thanks. Their names I have mentioned; their addresses, for obvious reasons, I have witheld.

SETON GORDON

AVIEMORE, INVERNESS-SHIRE

March 1927

SETON GORDON, LATER IN LIFE.
TAKEN BY ARTHUR W. FERGUSON, MAY 1964.

FOREWORD

I am honoured to write a foreword for this reprint of *Days with the Golden Eagle*; Seton Gordon's classic book on golden eagles is still relevant for today's readers. Eagles are long-lived birds and their ancestral hunting and nesting sites continue through the ages. Many of the eyrie sites that Seton Gordon visited in the early decades of the last century remain in use by golden eagles, as they were for centuries before even he first knew them. It is important that people interested in eagles understand the historical dimensions of this magnificent bird.

Even for a long-lived bird like the eagle, there is no possibility that any of those that he studied could still be alive today, but it is wonderful to think that the 'grandchildren' of some of them may be, for the oldest golden eagles in Scotland live to over thirty years. Interestingly, as I re-read his book I could also recognise the family names of keepers and stalkers, his contacts long ago, being the fathers or grandfathers of persons whom I have met while studying eagles in the last four decades.

Seton Gordon wrote this book while living at Aviemore. A very different Aviemore to that we see today! From his house, Achantoul (nowadays a Scottish Natural Heritage office), he could look out at the broad vista of the Cairngorms and see familiar corries and crags. Some of them are still used by eagles, but others, where he once wandered in solitude observing white hares, ptarmigan and eagles, are now busy and noisy with chairlifts and a mountain railway.

This book is about pioneering work. The long hours and days spent in cramped hides taking photographs with primitive and cumbersome equipment; the difficulties of processing and printing his photographs. How he would marvel at our new digital cameras that we can attach to our telescopes to obtain incredible images. Then there are his acute observations, many of them as accurate today and immediately recognisable to those who study eagles.

I was fortunate to meet Seton Gordon on several occasions when I was a young ornithologist in the Scottish Highlands. My memories include him asking me on several occasions about eagle nests that I had recently visited, and which he had known from half a century or more before. I also remember his tattered kilt, worn summer and winter with the dignity of a true Highland gentleman, and a mutual friend's story of the day he gave Seton a lift in his car from North Skye to Inverness – his longest journey ever – for the two pipers stopped at every opportunity to play a pibroch or a tune pertinent to the place.

At my home, I am pleased to have a memento of him – a small wooden pulley. On 8th May 1978, I discovered an eyrie in an ancient Scots pine in Glen Affric that had evaded me for years. It rested on two stout wooden beams laid across the branches – someone had built it. Later, I found out from an old stalker that the eagles' eyrie had collapsed in the 1930s and Seton had rebuilt the nest with some local men. The materials had been pulled up using the pulley. Some years later when ringing the eaglets, I found it on the ground when the rope had finally rotted.

Seton would be pleased to know that our eagle population is greater now than it was when he wrote his book. He would be disappointed, but probably not surprised, that eagles are still illegally killed. He would also be thrilled to know that each spring eagles still nest in the very places he knew a century ago. And long may they do so.

ROY DENNIS, MBE
STRATHSPEY
JANUARY 2003

INTRODUCTION

The debt I owe to Seton Gordon is not easily measured. It is quite possible that without him there would have been no nature writing tradition in Scotland at all, in which case, where would that have left those of us who came after, grateful for his footprints in the snow of our landscapes? The Victorian era into which he was born (in 1886) was characterised in Highland Scotland by a loathsome attitude towards wildlife in general and birds of prey in particular. Yet miraculously he emerged from it looking at golden eagles through camera and telescope rather than along the barrel of a shotgun, and with a personal crusade to communicate to others how an intimate acquaintance with wildest nature could be both a joy in itself and a great enrichment to the human mind. In the early years of the 20th century, this was new, daring work, and it must have won him as many enemies as admirers.

It also became his life's work. There are those who still speak with something approaching reverence of hearing him lecture inspirationally not long before his death at the age of 90.

Inspiration is a touchy subject among writers. I am often asked about the inspiration behind my own writing, and answer frankly that there is no such thing, that if you wait for inspiration to strike, you will write nothing. Instead, as this book so vividly demonstrates, there is the long slog of fieldwork, the frustration of our native weather, the draining of vast reserves of patience, the years of paying your dues by learning the ground and obeying nature's rules...all that and learning to use the tools and hone the writer's skills (and the photographer's in Seton Gordon's case)... and in return for all that, nature's reward is the sharing of a handful of secrets won painfully rather than inspirationally, and you must make of these what you can.

And then I must immediately qualify all of that by acknowledging a kind of inspiration, the only kind worth a damn, and that is the example of others who have gone before. In my book, then, Seton Gordon is a pre-eminent source of inspiration. Although I never met the man, he set me an example through his books of what a nature writer might achieve in Scotland, and how that work might be made relevant in the wider world.

It was John Muir who wrote that a man might be said to live on after his death through his books; the sentiment was never more truly appropriate than in the case of Seton Gordon and his most enduring titles – *The Cairngorm Hills of Scotland, The Charm of Skye, Amid Snowy Wastes, Afoot in Wild Places*...A good first edition of any one of these will change hands for £100 today. I believe the secret of their enduring appeal is that the best of his books are like intimate conversations with the man himself, not that you ever learn much about him, but rather so that he lends you his eyes and his unclouded vision of the wild world. It always comes as a shock to reach the end of one of his best books and remember how long ago they were written. Truly, the writer lives on after his death through his books.

That particular quality is nowhere more evident than in the pages of *Days with the Golden Eagle*. Seventy-five years after it was first published and almost a hundred years after its author took his first golden eagle photographs (April, 1904, he notes in an astounding aside in a later eagle book), and notwithstanding some period piece phraseology in the writing style, *Days with the Golden Eagle* re-emerges in this welcome new edition as fresh and vital and relevant as ever. Its authority is undiminished by time, many of its findings are unchallengeable even now because the whole thing is the fruit of astonishing labour. At the core of *Days with the Golden Eagle* is a study of twin eaglets in a tree eyrie. He christens them Cain and Abel because of the larger eaglet's relentless mauling of her smaller "brother", and the literature of Scottish nature writing offers up few more masterly-drawn nest-side accounts. Modern naturalists will raise more than eyebrows in protest that Seton Gordon and his wife Audrey (meticulously un-named in the book other than as "Mrs Seton Gordon") conducted their studies from a hide not 30 feet from the eyrie, but the revealed intimacy of the golden eagle nursery and the beauty of both prose and photography are fit tribute to the sensibilities of the watchers. It has simply never been better done.

There can be few more arduous studies in nature than the golden eagle, both for its wariness of people, and for the difficulty of the terrain where it chooses to nest (not to mention the frailties of the Highland climate). But if you have the stamina for it, there can be few more rewarding studies too, for it is a creature of exceptional powers and of quite remarkable and individualistic behaviour, and not a few mysteries. No-one who has succumbed to the lure of the golden eagle can deny their debt to Seton Gordon's work, and to this book in particular. No-one who travels restlessly among the landscapes of mountain and island trying to prise open his own small handful of nature's secrets to make what he can of them with a pen, can fail to notice in the books of Seton Gordon a dedication to the cause and a passionate respect for wildness that he too must honour and live up to.

My first full-length book, about the Cairngorms, leaned heavily on him. Even the title, *A High and Lonely Place,* was borrowed from his writing, a passage in his *The Cairngorm Hills of Scotland:*

> In the immense silences of these wild corries and dark rocks, the spirit of the high and lonely places revealed herself, so that one felt the serene and benign influence that has from time to time caused men to leave the society of their fellows and live on some remote surf-drenched isle – as St Cuthbert did on Farne – there to steep themselves in those spirirtual influences that are hard to receive in the crowded hours of human life…

The spirit of the high and lonely places is everywhere in the writings of Seton Gordon. But if you were to try and pin down the idea of that spirit as a single creature into which all the essences of wildness were distilled, might you not alight on the golden eagle? It seems to me now, after perhaps thirty years of reading Seton Gordon's books, that there was a kind of inevitability that someone like him would step forward from the Victorian killing fields and cry "Enough!", that it would occur to someone like him that there was a way back towards the old bonds between man and nature, that it mattered to someone like him to put the first footprints on what would prove a long hard road along which our own generations still toil.

For me, the appearance of this edition of *Days with the Golden Eagle* under the enlightened publishing imprint of Keith Whittles, is a cause for double celebration. Firstly it will put a masterpiece of Scottish nature writing before new generations of readers, and surely win new friends for the golden eagle and stimulate ideas there about the worth of wildness for its own sake. Secondly, I can look the world in the eye and say without a word of a lie that I have the same publisher as Seton Gordon.

JIM CRUMLEY
BALQUHIDDER
JANUARY 2003

CONTENTS

young eagle trying his wings J.C.Harrison

CHAPTER 1

SCOTTISH EYRIES OF THE GOLDEN EAGLE

"The whole air is a thoroughfare for the eagle." – EURIPIDES.

The golden eagle is supreme amongst British birds in the magnificent power and grace of its flight. It is undisputed chief of the aerial highways.

The soaring flight of the eagle above the high tops is a thing of great beauty. It seems – and probably is indeed true – that the bird could remain in the air hour after hour without the least weariness.

Before beginning to tell of the ways of eagles in the Scottish Highlands, I will give a short description of the golden eagle for the convenience of those not acquainted with the "king of birds" at close quarters.

The hen bird is the larger of the two, and weighs between 10 and 13 pounds. (A cock golden eagle, about nine months old, was found by Mr Macleay, taxidermist, Inverness, to weigh 8 pounds

2 ounces.) The wing-spread is from 5 to 8 feet, but Yarrell and other standard works on British birds record that an eagle shot at Warkworth in 1735 had a wing-spread of 11 feet 3 inches! The plumage of cock and hen is alike, but the adult plumage is not acquired till the bird is four years old. The mature plumage is the same winter and summer, but in old birds often has a bleached look towards the end of the breeding season. The feathers of the head and neck are bright rufous brown, the tips and edges being bright tawny buff, which causes the golden appearance. The whole of the back is dark chestnut brown, but the bases of the feathers are white. The under parts, tall, and wing-feathers are lighter brown with a good deal of grey mottling. The legs are feathered down to and including the tarsus with rufous brown feathers with dark shafts. The bill is black, and greyish at the base; the toes are a rich yellow, and claws black.

In the immature plumage the head and neck are not so golden; the rest of the bird is much darker brown, but there is more white showing on the under parts and on the tail and under the wings. The young bird can be distinguished by the whiter tail with a black band at the tip.

In its nesting the eagle differs from other birds, most of which build a new home every spring. A pair of eagles own, on an average, two, or possibly three eyries. These eyries are used alternately, and as an eyrie is added to each time it is occupied, in the course of years it becomes an enormous structure.

In the Western Highlands a rock is generally chosen as a nesting site, but in the Central and Eastern Highlands a tree is often used The tree is usually an old Scots fir, but I know of two eyries in birch trees.

Eagles rarely nest in high precipices; sometimes the eyrie is easily accessible, and one eyrie that I know is actually on the ground below a rock.

In Scotland the golden eagle does not often nest at high levels, because the snows of winter are still covering the rocks at the season of its nest-building. I know of one eyrie just 3000 feet above the sea, and there is a reputed nest which must be 3500 feet high; but in the Central Highlands the eyrie is generally from 1500 to 2500 feet above sea-level, and in the west it may be only a few hundred feet above the waters of the Atlantic.

The golden eagle is an early nester. I have seen an eagle carrying a large fir branch towards the eyrie on the 27th day of January, but February is the usual month when nest-building is commenced. In the pine forests the eagle constructs her eyrie of pine branches throughout. She makes the foundation of large branches and the upper parts of green pine-shoots, which she always breaks from the trees, tearing them off with her powerful bill. She lines her eyrie usually with a grass-like plant known as *Luzula sylvatica,* and flies long distances for it. But if she cannot find it she makes shift with heather-shoots and, perhaps, tufts of hill grasses, or she may add shoots of bearberry and cranberry.

The eggs usually number two. I have seen a good many eyries, but have never found three eggs, although clutches of three are on record (see Chapter 6). The first egg seems to be laid several days before the second, and as the eagle commences to sit directly she has laid her first egg, the first-hatched eaglet has a good start in the world.

The first-laid egg seems to be the more lightly marked of the two, and the second egg, has rich markings of red-brown. Perhaps the oviduct is stimulated to produce colouring matter by the passing of the first egg. A golden eagle's egg, is about the size of a goose's, but is rounder and much thicker shelled.

I am doubtful if the cock eagle broods the eggs, but he takes his turn at brooding the eaglets when they are very young.

I will first describe an eyrie in an old Scots pine in the Central Highlands. The tree is at the foot of a hill, and is well sheltered, and thus the eagles nest early. A few years ago I visited the nest in mid-March. The weather was summer-like, but snow lay unbroken upon the higher hills, and even beside the eyrie large drifts were lying below the trees. The eagle was already brooding on her nest. She had laid only one egg, but was sitting closely. She was so sound asleep that I was obliged to whistle to arouse her. After the first few whistles I noticed a head peer sleepily over the side of the nest to see what the noise was about, and then the great bird, without undue haste, rose to her feet, walked to the edge of the eyrie, and spread her dark sails to the breeze.

One sunny day when I was watching an eyrie in a fir tree the eagle flew from the nest high into the air, perhaps to stretch herself and enjoy the warm sunshine. She caused panic among the grouse near, which immediately rose in a body and scattered, flying at their topmost speed over the brow of the hill. Soon the eagle returned to her eyrie, and fell so soundly asleep that even when I stood below the tree and whistled she did not at first hear me.

If the eagle's eyrie is on so steep a hillside that it is possible to approach closely without alarming the bird, and then suddenly look at her from *above*, she is far more frightened than if she sees the intruder beneath her, and by visiting the eyrie from above one is more likely to cause her to desert her eggs.

The eyrie of which I write here has had a curious history. For at least fifteen years it was in regular use. Then one winter a heavy snowstorm caused it to fall, but it was caught upon a large branch a few feet below its original position. In the spring the eagles, apparently not noticing the change, occupied the eyrie as before.

The eagle as she broods on her eyrie in this country of wild primeval forest has an inspiring view. She looks across to the high tops and sees the early morning sun flood the snowy slopes with rosy light. She hears from the forest below her the soft bubbling notes of the amorous blackcock at their fighting-ground, and the wild clarion call of the missel-thrush as he greets the April dawn. Other sounds she hears: the hoarse bark of a hind, the curious sneezing cry of a capercaillie on some pine tree, the distant melody of curlew and golden plover on the brown moorland, the becking of a cock grouse as he shakes the frosty dew from his plumage. I remember once spending a night beside an eagle at the eyrie and seeing the first sun-flush burn upon her golden head, so that it was no longer golden but deep rose coloured; and so I like to picture that lonely eyrie on many calm, sunny dawns when spring is young and when all the life of the lonely upland places is commencing slowly to stir to the increasing power of the sun.

Then there are days when the noontide sun shines full into the eyrie; when, even in April, the forest seems to burn with a fierce, dry heat; when the red ants swarm up and down the eagle's tree, and each large, conical ant-bill is a mass of seething, feverish life. There are days, too, in April when the black wind from the north brings with it dry, powdery snow which drifts across the moorland at the fringe of the forest, and the pines commence to droop beneath their mantle of soft, clinging white. From time to time the eagle rises on her nest and shakes the snow from her dark plumage, then gazes fiercely over the dim world of white that might be some Polar waste from the bitter cold of the wind and the grey masses of fast-driven snow.

I shall always remember one April day climbing to an eyrie that was built in a wild gorge 2000 feet above sea-level. Even in the glen there had been a heavy snowstorm, and on the hill two feet of snow covered the ground so that walking was a slow and laborious thing. After what seemed to be an interminable climb I reached the wind-swept gorge at the top of the pass and saw the eagle rise from the nest. The cup of the eyrie was the one spot on all that hill which was snow-free. A full twelve inches of snow covered the fringes of the eyrie, and the eagle must have been brooding to keep her nest free of snow for the eggs which would shortly be laid there – the eyrie was empty then, but there were two eggs in it a week later. Had there been a strong wind at the time of this heavy snowfall the eyrie would have been drifted up and the eagle obliged to desert it. A tree-nesting eagle never runs this danger; she can always keep her eyrie free of snow, and her chief danger is wind. However well constructed a tree-eyrie may be, there is always a possibility that a fierce gale may dash it to the ground. Not many years ago an eyrie was lost in this way just after the eggs were laid. Although the eggs were fresh the birds did not nest again that season, for it seems to be a very rare thing for a golden eagle to lay twice in the same year. Only last summer the existence of an eyrie was proved by the discovery of it lying on the ground. It had evidently been used for many years, and although I had always felt sure that the birds were nesting in that glen, there were so many trees that it was difficult to search them all, and thus the existence of this tree-eyrie remained unknown until it came to grief.

But let us return to the eyrie beneath the hill at the fringes of the forest. The first time I saw that eyrie was many years ago now, but the stalker who showed it to me – a delightful man he was – is still keen and energetic as ever. The nest, although not very high in the tree, was hard to reach, because the tree trunk was large and without branches, and so we returned home and fetched a ladder, which we carried up to the eyrie. We hoped that our troubles were now over, but on climbing the ladder I found that I was still about three feet below the level of the eyrie. That stalker was a strong man. He lifted the ladder, with me at the top of it, until it rested against his chest, and held me thus while I focussed my camera and obtained the best photograph I have ever taken of a golden eagle's eyrie.

This eagle brought some curious prey to her young. I remember one day finding a stoat in the eyrie, perhaps the very last thing one would expect to see in an eagle's nest.

It was this same eagle that met disaster from her house taking fire a few years later. She had, as is usual, two eyries, and the one in the tree was used alternately with the nest on the cliff above.

A second pair – perhaps the progeny of these birds – have their nest on a rock a few miles to the eastward. A curious mishap befell the eaglets in that eyrie one year. I suspect that during a tremendous battle the two youngsters overbalanced and fell to the ground below. It is possible that one of them was killed by the fall, or that the stronger of the two made an end of its fellow on the ground. At all events, when the stalker and I visited the eyrie we found the nest empty and one of the eaglets on the heather below the cliff. It had fallen at least thirty feet, but was alive and well, and the parent birds had built a small new eyrie round it. I frequently visited that eaglet, and it gradually came to know me and would feed from my hand, even sampling a piece of banana peel which I offered it. As it became fledged it used to wander a little way over the hillside. I remember how interested it was in the red ants which walked up and down its legs, and how it watched a butterfly with much curiosity. It was the parent of that eaglet who carried up to her eyrie a large red rubber ring, having evidently a nice sense of colour, and believing that the red ring showed off the green branches of her eyrie! On more than one occasion since then I have found a bamboo stick in an eyrie. Another pair of eagles were in the habit of bringing to their eyrie, even when the eaglets were well grown, fresh shoots of raspberry at intervals of a few days.

Eagles are shy birds, but their affection for an old-established eyrie is shown by the following. On a hillside in the Central Highlands a pair of eagles have had their eyrie for many years. During the War Canadian foresters felled large areas of the old Caledonian pine forest, and among them the hillside on the eagles' tree was growing. They considerately left the tree, but from being one of many it is now a conspicuous object. The Forestry

A YOUNG EAGLET IN A ROCK EYRIE.

Commission since the War have acquired the estate. They have put up a bothy a few hundred yards from the ancestral home of the eagles, and here seven or eight men live. Notwithstanding this the eagles attempted to nest here a couple of years ago. In doing this they showed a faith that was almost pathetic, because one of the men employed on the estate makes a considerable income every year in taking egg collectors to eagles' eyries. Here was a nest literally under his very nose! Need it be added that this pair of eagles reared no family that season?

In former years the golden eagle nested on North Uist, one of the Outer Hebrides. There were numbers of cats straying over the island moors, and the eagles preyed upon them and carried them to the nest. The true wild cat is on the increase in the Highlands at the present day, and it will be interesting to see whether the eagles will take to bringing them to the eyrie – although a wild cat is a much more formidable animal than a domestic cat that has become wild.

The soaring powers of the golden eagle are well known, but what I witnessed one April day will be believed with difficulty. I was standing on a hill slope just above a pine forest where a pair of golden eagles have their nest each year. The day was bitterly cold, and a strong breeze from the north was bringing heavy snow showers to the glen, while on the high tops the drifting snow was whirled high into the air. As I stood there the eagle's mate came over the ridge. He was flying low, but on seeing me commenced to mount. Leaning upon the wind he rose higher and higher. There was no perceptible movement of his dark wings, yet he mounted until he was invisible to the eye. The glass still revealed him – a dark speck against the blue vault of the sky – then some clouds crossed and hid him from my view, for he was far above them. What height must he have reached when he was invisible to my unaided eye ? It is of course impossible to do more than surmise, but in the autumn of 1926 I was on Sgurr nan Gillean, one of the Black Cuillin of Skye, when an eagle rose from his perch on the topmost pinnacle and sailed above me. Knowing my own height and the height of the hill-top, I was able accurately to judge his distance above me, and at an elevation of 1500 feet he seemed quite a large bird. And so I would say that for the eagle to be invisible to the unaided eye he must be 8000 feet above the observer.

Although my own experience was an interesting one, a stalker friend of mine, John McIntosh, who was for some seasons watcher at the Corrour Bothy in the Forest of Mar, saw an eagle climb even higher than I did. The weather had been intensely hot on the Cairngorms, and then one day the north wind brought cool air to the hills. McIntosh happened to see a golden eagle soar out from its ledge of rock and "put the glass on to it," as they say in stalking language. This eagle, too, mounted serenely and without effort into the wind, and at last was so small that McIntosh could not see it with his unaided eye. But his glass for a time brought it nearer, and then even in the field of the telescope the bird was invisible. When it is remembered that a stalking-glass magnifies an object at least twenty-five times, it shows to what a great altitude that eagle had soared. It must have been at least ten thousand feet above the rock from which it took wing.

How astonishing that a bird of such splendid flight should allow itself to be mobbed by the impudent grey crows that live with it in the old pine forests! The crows seem to have a great hatred of the King of Birds. Often one sees an eagle sailing overhead with a grey crow in close pursuit; sometimes a pair of these birds are the aggressors, and with harsh "craas" swoop and dive at the eagle. But the eagle invariably ignores their attacks and sails on his way serenely. He evidently thinks the hoodies are entirely beneath notice.

Far up a lonely corrie of a western deer forest a pair of golden eagles have their two eyries. Both nests are built upon ledges of rock, but one of them has not been occupied for a number of years. I discovered the eyrie now in use in an interesting way. One day at the very end of March I crossed the ridge and looked into the corrie. The sun was strong but a bitter nor'-easter was sweeping up the corrie, and each small waterfall on the cliffs was a mass of ice. Near the corrie some stalker or shepherd must have set fire to the hill grass and then gone his way, for the hillside was smouldering but no one was in sight. I was convinced the eagle was nesting in the corrie, but at the time the only eyrie I knew of was the unoccupied one. As I passed it, therefore, I looked across at it carefully through my telescope, but it was derelict – quite flat and with ice and snow all about it. But as I sat quietly in a sunny and sheltered spot I saw a dark speck appear in the blue of the sky above the hillside opposite. The speck soon resolved itself into a golden eagle. On half-closed wings she slanted earthward at great speed, entered the corrie and, not noticing me, alighted on her eyrie quite near.

The nest was difficult to see, and I do not think I should have found it had it not been for her opportune arrival. At first I could not understand her absence from her eggs on a day of such bitter wind, and then it occurred to me that she had been disturbed by the stalker, or the hill fire he had kindled, and was now returning to her eyrie believing that the danger had passed.

I walked quietly along the foot of the cliff, but unfortunately, when I had reached a point about a hundred yards from the eyrie, the warm sun on the cliff dislodged some giant icicles which fell with a splintering crash. The eagle, much startled, looked out over the edge of the nest, saw me below, and sprang into space. The nest was not more than ten feet from the foot of the cliff, and could be climbed to without much difficulty. It was not a large or a bulky eyrie. Since there were no fir trees in the neighbourhood, the eagle had built her nest of large sticks of birch. The eyrie was lined with heather and a large spray of crowberry (*Empetrum*), and at the outside of the lining lay the dried stem and flower-head of a tansy-like plant.

Two eggs were in the eyrie, one of them (as usual) richly spotted with red-brown, the other almost white.

At the foot of the cliff were two or three plants of the purple mountain saxifrage. This saxifrage is first of all hill plants to blossom, and although the grass was brown as in midwinter, its delightful crimson flowers were already fully opened, and gave a touch of singular beauty to the cliffs of that wild corrie.

Very different was the weather when I visited another rock eyrie of the golden eagle one day in July. The day had been hot with constant sunshine, and I climbed from the glen through the short hours of night to the corrie, where the eagles had their eyrie at a height of about 2700 feet above the sea. In the glen the air at midnight had been cool, but as I climbed I reached the layer of heated air that had risen at sunset, and at 2500 feet it was far warmer than it had been 1000 feet lower. The air at dawn was heavy with the delightful scent of the growing things of the hills: the scent of the cow-wheat, the wild thyme, the young ling, the crowberry. I shall always remember reaching the lonely corrie of the eagles at sunrise and seeing, against the deep blue sky, the young eagle, fully feathered, seeming to greet the coming day. He had walked from the eyrie (it was built on a small rock) and was standing on a steep heathery slope awaiting the arrival of one of his parents with breakfast. Far below him in the corrie were herds of red deer; above him, on the ridge, was a white-winged mother ptarmigan with her brood.

That same pair of eagles had their eyrie some years later on a rock within a few hundred yards of the main road from Perth to Braemar, and the roadmen told me that they had frequently seen the birds carrying food to the eaglets.

CHAPTER 2

A PAIR OF EAGLES AND THEIR HOME LIFE

THE FIRST FOUR WEEKS

" As an eagle stirreth up her nest, fluttereth over her young, spreadeth abroad her wings, taketh them, beareth them on her wings." Deuteronomy xxxii. II.

It was one of those rare April days when the sun shines with summer warmth and the air is soft and mild. There was no breeze in the old pine forest, and the ancient, heavy-crowned trees seemed to hold their green branches eagerly towards the strong sunlight.

All at once, high in the blue vault of heaven, I saw the form of a golden eagle sailing serenely above the forest. From the fringe of the woodlands a few grouse rose terrified at her approach and scattered wildly. She heeded them not, but as she half turned in her flight the sun shone full upon the golden plumage of her neck, and she became a veritable eagle of burnished gold. For a time she sailed thus above the forest, then suddenly steered eastward as though forming some resolve and, closing her great wings, shot like a thunderbolt to the trees of a steep hill-face about a mile from where I stood.

I thought it possible, since the afternoon had been so unusually warm and sunny, that she had been "off duty" for a time and had swept down on to her eyrie.

My wife was with me at the time, and accordingly the two of us commenced to walk in as straight a line as possible in the direction where the eagle had disappeared.

We arrived, after much strenuous climbing through long heather and close-growing pines, at the spot where we judged the eagle had entered the wood, yet no nest was visible. But in order to make certain that she should not be sitting concealed in her eyrie I clapped my hands, and, not fifty yards from us, the eagle spread her great wings and launched herself into space. There was still no eyrie visible to us, but on climbing the steep hillside we soon saw it. The nest was built upon the crown of a very old Scots pine, and was so large that it covered the whole of the crown of the tree. It had evidently been used for many years, and at the foot of the tree lay the remains of a *still earlier* eyrie, so ancient and disintegrated that it had resolved itself into the earth and become a mound of soil, moss, and sticks.

I believe that the tree had been the nesting-site of that pair of eagles or their ancestors for a full fifty years, and probably much longer.

The eyrie in use was an enormous structure, 6 to 8 feet in diameter and some 4 feet in depth. It was built of pine branches, and the top and cup of the nest were formed of small fir branches, fresh and green, that had been torn by the eagles from the trees of the forest. In the nest lay two eggs, one richly marked with red spots and blotches, the other white and almost unspotted.

We gathered a few branches and bunches of heather and set them up on the hillside about thirty feet from the nest to form the nucleus of a hiding-place, for the hill rose so steeply that at that distance from the eyrie we were almost level with the top of the nest. Accordingly, we judged that from here we should be able to photograph the home life of the eagles when the opportune moment arrived.

For no less than five weeks the eagle broods her eggs, and since it was inadvisable to disturb her until her family were hatched out, we kept away from the eyrie until the tenth day of May.

The spring that year had been unusually severe, and in the early days of May the trees of the forest had been snow-covered and the ground each night had been bound by frost. But the sun shone warm as I walked beside a loch of the forest, and the greenshank made wild music overhead. The loch lay calm and still. Trees, hill, and the idly drifting clouds were all faithfully mirrored on its surface, where wigeon swam and goosanders dived for their dinner of trout. Where pine and birch grew together, the pale green of the opening buds of the birch blended with the more sombre needles of the pines. All around rose snowy hills, their white slopes dazzling in the strong May sunlight, but in the glen the scent of the young birch foliage filled the air, and one felt that summer was at hand.

I had scarcely left the glen when an eagle rose from one of the fir trees on the steep hillside above me. He – for I imagine it was the cock – had been perched perhaps a hundred yards from the nest; his mate a little later rose from the eyrie itself. I felt convinced that the eggs had escaped the collectors, who were so numerous in the locality, and that the eaglets had been hatched, because when the hen is sitting on eggs the cock is very rarely seen beside the nest. When I reached the hillside above the nest and looked into the eyrie I saw there two eaglets, from eight to ten days old.

From birth the young hen eaglet is the larger of the two, and there is no doubt that she sometimes kills her brother during the first five weeks of their lives in the eyrie. On this May afternoon the young hen was deliberately aiming blow after blow at her unfortunate brother when I arrived at the nest. I added to the pile of branches which were to conceal our "hide," and then left the hill, while down in the glen below wood-warblers, redstarts, and tree-pipits were singing their welcome to the summer sunshine.

Three days later we carried a small hiding-tent up the hill and placed it in position before the nest, covering it carefully over with the fir branches and heather already heaped there so that no canvas showed through. I took first "watch" and entered the hide at 11.30 a.m. The eaglets had grown considerably during the three days since last I had seen them. In the nest lay a freshly plucked grouse. During the morning the chicks often flapped their tiny stumps of

An eaglet in a rock eyrie, about four weeks old.

wings and preened their white down. Once the young hen called loudly, then gave her brother a vicious blow on the head with her sharp bill. At 2.50 p.m. the young hen felled the cock with two or three well-directed blows, and at 3 p.m. she again attacked him.

During my five and a half hours' watch I did not once see either eagle come to the eyrie, but my peep-hole, cut in the canvas of the hiding-tent, was so small that it was impossible to keep my eye glued to it continually, and I believe that the cock must have come twice to the eyrie unperceived by me, for when I left the hide there were two more grouse in the nest.

The following day the eyrie was left undisturbed, but when, on the 15th of May, my wife took the watch she had no better luck. The eagles seemed to be suspicious – perhaps as they soared at a great height above the nest they saw the canvas of the hiding tent through the covering branches, or perhaps it was simply that they resented seeing human beings in their glen – for our approach to the eyrie could be watched by them when we were still a mile away.

I must here mention that during our first few watches my wife and I always approached the eyrie together, and whoever did not take the watch walked away as ostentatiously as possible, in order to distract the attention of the parent eagles. But after a few days we found it possible to go unaccompanied to the hide. The eagle on duty at the time sailed away while the intruder was as yet a mile or so from the nest, and flew right out of sight, and as the eyrie was in thick forest the eagle could never be sure when we left the nest, or even if we went to it at all. Accordingly, after an absence of perhaps an hour and a half the great bird would return, and, provided the person on watch was well concealed in the hiding-tent by that time, take it for granted that all was well. But on one occasion it was as well that a friend accompanied me, for when we reached the nest both parent eagles were soaring high overhead, and must have seen our arrival. In order to mislead them, my friend at once walked on in their full view while I crept hastily into the hide.

It was fortunate that it was usually unnecessary for us to go together to the eyrie, for it saved the person who was not on duty a tedious climb, and in this way we were able to spend alternate days in the hide, whereas if it had been essential for both of us to go each day we should not have been able to keep such a regular daily watch.

In photographing most birds from a hiding-tent it is necessary that two persons together, or sometimes three, approach the already erected hiding-place. One observer enters the hide; the others walk on, thus misleading the bird, which thinks vaguely of human beings as abstract danger or perhaps is unable to count. Accordingly, if the bird is already used to the erection which forms the hiding-place, it waits till the accomplices are out of sight and then returns to the nest with no suspicions that a human being may be concealed somewhere near. It must also be remembered that birds (with the possible exception of some geese) have no smell. But, as I have explained, the wary golden eagle always flew away so far, and left the eyrie when the photographer was such a long distance off, that it was unnecessary for my wife and I to go to the nest together. It would probably have been quite different if we had been watching a rock eyrie in an open glen, for then the eagle would have seen with its keen eye from some distant mountain-top all that happened near its eyrie.

Although the eaglets were only a fortnight old and had as yet no rudiments of feathers upon them, they seemed impervious to the cold wind. On this day the weariness of sitting for six hours in a cramped position, looking through a small hole with one eye, was lessened by the life-and-death battle between the two eaglets. The larger of the two tormented her smaller brother, pecking him without mercy and several times driving him almost to the edge of the eyrie. There, just as he seemed about to fall, she caught him with her bill and swung him back into the centre of the eyrie. The fate of the weaker eaglet indeed hung in the balance at this time, and since the young hen seemed bent on killing her brother we named her Cain and her brother Abel.

As the parent eagles appeared to be suspicious of us and the hide, we decided to give them five days' rest from our intrusion, and returned to the eyrie on 20th May fully expecting to find Abel no longer there; but to our relief he had survived his bad usage, largely, we felt sure, owing to his greater agility. When we were perhaps half a mile from the eyrie the mother eagle sailed out from the nest, and just as I was about to enter the hide the cock swept past in a magnificent curve. He had been hunting on the high hills, and when he saw us beside the nest shot up into the air again, at the same time dropping the grouse or ptarmigan he was carrying home to his family. The bird fell into deep heather some hundreds of yards below us, and we were unable to find it. In the eyrie were the remains of a hare and the wings and skeleton of a jackdaw or hoodie-crow.

Despite the fact that we had been seen near the eyrie by the parent eagles, I entered the hide at 4.20 p.m., and my wife, accompanied by our collie dog, ostentatiously left the corrie in order to distract the attention of the eagles.

The day was still and very warm. In the soft, silent air was the scent of young birches and growing blaeberry plants. The forest dozed contentedly in summer warmth after the long winter and tardy spring.

The eaglets, too, slept.

Heavy clouds drifted across from the hills towards evening. It became very dark, and a thunderstorm seemed to be approaching. But after a few drops of rain the clouds drifted over, and as the air became less oppressive the eaglets roused themselves and stood up in the eyrie to preen their down.

At last, at twenty minutes past six in the evening, I had my first view of the mother eagle at close quarters. There was a sudden rush, and she alighted at the edge of the eyrie, eyed the camera lens (which projected a fraction of an inch beyond the front of the hide) for a moment, then, her suspicions allayed, picked up a large fir branch and rearranged it carefully. She then proceeded to feed each chick in turn on the hare. She gave them small pieces of flesh, and with great relish swallowed large pieces of bone herself.

When the eaglets had been satisfied she took up her position beside them, standing motionless on guard at the edge of the eyrie.

I think she had settled herself for the night, but just after eight o'clock, when dusk was veiling the hill, she seemed to hear some sound far below her and glided silently from the eyrie.

At once, unseen by her, I left the hide and hurried to the glen, where I learnt that my wife had made our collie bark in order to cause the eagle to leave the eyrie, thinking that otherwise I should have been obliged to remain in the hide all night – for it would have been fatal to have let the eagle see me emerge from the hide so close to her, as this would have made her suspicious of it for always.

We pitched our tent that night in the forest, amongst junipers and pines and sweet-scented birches, and at half-past six the next morning, 21st May, my wife commenced her first watch in the hide since our two first fruitless days.

It was a delightful morning. A cool breeze from the west stirred the birches, and soft white clouds drifted across the deep blue sky. Upon the south-facing slopes the sun shone golden, but there was deep shade upon the steep hill-face where the eaglets lay in their eyrie.

Two hours after I had left her in the hide my wife saw the cock eagle sweep in from the east and alight on the edge of the nest. He fed both the young in turn on a grouse. Although we did not realise it at the time, this was an unusual thing for him to do, for he left the feeding of the family almost entirely to his mate.

At 11.30 a.m. we changed over and I commenced a long watch.

By eleven o'clock the sun had climbed above the steep slope that rose southwards above the eyrie and shone full into the nest. In the fierce rays the eaglets gasped and panted, and seemed grateful when passing clouds momentarily hid the sun.

At ten minutes to one the cock eagle alighted on the nest with a plucked grouse or ptarmigan held firmly in one foot. For two minutes he stood motionless in a magnificent attitude, heedless of the eaglets' yelping cries for food.

His head and neck were almost white, and all over he was much lighter than the hen in plumage. It was interesting to see how much smaller he was than his mate.

It was a delight to watch him as he stood there, his eyes flashing with pride and strength, his every gesture regal.

The plumage on his legs was extraordinarily thick, giving the impression that he was wearing the "Oxford trousers" so fashionable at that particular period.

Suddenly, to the disappointment of his brood, he sprang into space, and there was quietness in the eyrie for an hour. Then one of the parents sailed past overhead and Cain yelped loudly. She evidently expected to be fed, but when neither parent appeared she commenced to peck feebly at the legs of the grouse the cock had brought, and a little later on attempted to swallow a thin bone. Her brother Abel meanwhile lay miserably in the nest, cheeping incessantly for food.

Cain seemed to reason thus: "Even if dinner *is* late there is always one game I can play," and deliberately walked across to

Abel, aiming careful and oft-repeated blows at his bare "behind." After the first few blows the unfortunate victim jumped to his feet and fled miserably to the edge of the eyrie, where he lay down. But Cain relentlessly pursued him, and struck several blows at his back. Again Abel retreated in terror, and Cain, tiring of her sport, left him this time in peace, and, probably for the first time in her life, actually commenced to tear up a grouse for herself. The eaglets were now about three weeks old.

It was not until five minutes past five in the afternoon that the mother eagle alighted at the eyrie. She at once commenced to feed Cain, who was very hungry and excited, but poor Abel continued to lie dejectedly in the nest and did not attempt to walk towards her. At last it seemed to occur to his mother that he too should be fed, for she leaned across to him and he took from her bill, still with dejected mien, some half-dozen mouthfuls of grouse, then lay down again and refused more food.

Perhaps he felt the effects of his recent bad usage!

For an hour and a quarter the mother eagle remained at the eyrie, and during much of this time she fed Cain, who consumed an astonishing amount of meat for one so small. Her crop bulged more and more, until it seemed as though it must burst, and still she accepted complacently the food her mother continued to offer. From time to time this gorged and self-satisfied eaglet looked down with contempt (so it seemed to me) upon poor Abel lying beside her without appetite. Once the mother eagle gave Cain a quite large bone. The eaglet almost choked the first time she tried to swallow this, but at the second attempt the bone disappeared successfully.

At last the eaglet was so gorged she was unable to swallow even the choicest morsel of grouse, and then her mother herself gulped down the entrails, which hung in long ribbons from her bill as she gobbled them up with evident delight, reminding one of an expert macaroni consumer! At last she spread her dark wings and vanished from my sight.

Five days later, 26th May, as I was climbing to the eyrie I saw one of the eagles fly past, and seeing me, sheer off, carrying in one foot a plucked ptarmigan or grouse.

The eaglets were now about twenty-six days old, and Cain was already growing the wing and tail feathers, which looked like a black edging to her wing and tail stumps. Abel was also growing finely, and a recent heavy meal had swelled his crop. For an hour and a half the eaglets were quiet, then Cain rose and stood menacingly over Abel, who sullenly awaited the attack. But the bully now appeared to treat her brother with more respect, and on this occasion she aimed no blows upon him.

At ten minutes past one that day Cain, who was always more alert than Abel, commenced to cheep excitedly. A minute later the cock eagle arrived from his hunting. In one foot he held a plucked grouse, but as usual did not attempt to feed the eaglets, and anon sprang out into space. From 3 p.m. to 6.30 p.m. my wife took the watch, but neither of the parent eagles came, although both eaglets were evidently very hungry and called constantly for their mother to come and feed them on the grouse the cock had brought. The tedium of the watch this day was banished by listening to all the different birds which could be heard from the hide – singing or going about their business. The birds heard included a redstart, who habitually sang from a perch on the branches actually comprising the hide, and who had a nest near by; other birds heard were goldcrest, crested tit, ring-ouzel, missel-thrush, curlew, greenshank, cole-tit, wren, chaffinch, willow-warbler, woodcock, red grouse, song-thrush, cuckoo, lesser black-backed gull, and stonechat.

The last few days of May brought wild weather to the eagles' country.

A BIRD'S-EYE VIEW OF THE EYRIE OF CAIN AND ABEL.

CHAPTER 3

A PAIR OF EAGLES AND THEIR HOME LIFE

ABEL SURVIVES HIS ILL-TREATMENT

On the 28th of May the sun shone as I climbed the steep hill, but on the far side of the glen heavy showers were drifting eastward across the valley and a black stormcloud hid Ben Nevis from view. At one o'clock in the afternoon, after I had been in the hide for an hour and a half, a fierce squall of rain and hail swept down upon the eyrie from the west. When the storm was at its height the mother eagle alighted at her home. With deliberation she walked to the windward side of the eyrie and stood so that she sheltered her young. And then as the storm became, if possible, more fierce, she walked across to the eaglets and brooded them. The two eaglets lay together happy and quiet. After a time one of them tapped upon her bill, and to this child she gave a kiss – or its equivalent.

23

The eagle made a magnificent picture as she brooded her young in deep gloom, while the wind rushed through the pines and in the glen far below the sunlight gleamed. The eyrie swayed rhythmically in the gale; on the roof and weather side of the hiding-tent the rain and hail rattled like small-shot. The eagle's tawny plumage became matted with moisture, and from her bill the raindrops fell in a steady drip.

In half an hour the rain ceased, and the eagle immediately left the nest. Five minutes later the sun shone brilliantly on the eyrie, and the eaglets slept peacefully, while on the clean, rain-washed air the scent of birch trees was drifted across to me.

After an interval of about an hour the mother eagle again alighted on the eyrie and for three-quarters of an hour fed her family. She gorged Cain before paying the slightest attention to Abel, who all the time lay in the cup of the eyrie cheeping miserably for his share of dinner. When at last his mother turned her attention to him she found him moodily pecking at a bone, feeling, evidently, that no one loved him. He was so depressed by his mother's neglect of him that he ignored for a time the morsel of grouse which she held out towards him in her bill. After she had at length induced Abel to swallow a few mouthfuls of food she took up her position at the edge of the eyrie, watching for her mate. The sun shone full upon her splendid golden head; as she felt the gusts of wind strike her she pressed down her great tail against the nest, the better to balance herself.

For just over an hour she stood there, her stern glance sweeping the glen below in search of her mate. As he did not come she sailed out into the wind to look for him.

Since almost all birds stand head to wind, I was interested to see that the eagle during fully half the time she was standing at the eyrie had her back to the breeze, which ruffled the feathers of her head into a crest.

The eaglets, with distended crops, lay together in the nest, Cain with one wing over Abel as though protecting him. After a time the mother eagle flew up again to see that all was well. She at once picked up a branch in her bill and rearranged it in the nest. Then, after lifting the remains of a hare from the floor of the eyrie, she spread her wings and sailed out to search once more for her missing mate.

I had already been in the hide for six hours, and so when she had gone I crawled out of my place of concealment, so stiff and cold that I found it hard to stand erect.

I had scarcely left the eyrie when a violent squall of rain accompanied by blinding wind swept across from the west, and I thought of the eagle returning swiftly to her nest through the gathering gloom and brooding the eaglets during the moonless night while the wind rushed through the swaying pines and the eyrie rocked like a vessel in a storm. The following day, 29th May, my wife took the morning watch from 8 a.m. to 1 p.m.

After two hours the hen arrived, but left immediately. She returned after an hour and a quarter with a large green pine branch, which she arranged carefully at the edge of the eyrie. Immediately she had left the cock arrived; he also had a branch, and after arranging it to his satisfaction he plucked a hare or rabbit lying in the bottom of the nest and threw away the fur over his shoulder. In spite of urgent cries from the eaglets he did not feed them, and soon left the eyrie. At one o'clock I entered the hide, and at twenty minutes past one, at the beginning of a squall, the hen eagle arrived. Cain immediately ran to her for shelter, but Abel, wrapped up in his miserable musings, ignored her arrival.

For the duration of the squall the mother brooded the eaglets, then commenced to feed them, and continued to do so for three-quarters of an hour. I was glad to see that this time she fed Abel first, although Cain as usual attempted to keep her small brother in the background. The eaglets' meal on this occasion consisted of a course of grouse followed by hare – a meal fit for a king!

Sometimes one of the eaglets was slow in swallowing a morsel of hare, and then the mother eagle at once passed it on to the other youngster.

After a really good meal Abel was in excellent form, and when a little later on Cain attempted to bully him by pecking at him, Abel, to my astonishment, actually retaliated, and to such purpose that Cain was forced to run to the far side of the nest!

The wind roared through the pines as the family was being fed, and the mother eagle, standing on the edge of the eyrie, balanced herself like a sailor on the deck of a rolling vessel. During this meal the eagle ate little herself, but sometimes when an eaglet seized a large lump of meat before it had been torn into small pieces, she first permitted the youngster to try to swallow it, then gently took it from the eaglet, tore it up, and swallowed some of it herself. After dinner the eaglets played with small sticks and a feather, and altogether were very pleased with life.

The eagle was absent a short time from the eyrie, then returned with a bunch of heather, placing it in the nest. Almost at once a gust of wind swept it away, and she watched it go with indifference, but soon sailed out over the corrie, in half an hour returning with a green fir branch in her bill. She laid this branch upon the eyrie and at once took wing. Five minutes afterwards I saw a shadow cross the hide, and a second later she again alighted, bringing with her another fir branch. Again she took wing and again alighted in the space of five minutes, and commenced to feed the eaglets on the remains of the hare, offering them titbits in turn for half an hour. Then she left.

At twelve minutes past three the cock arrived with a grouse. He remained at the eyrie only two minutes, and left the plucked grouse with its feet sticking up. Before he sprang into the air he looked with obvious pride at one of the eaglets moving a large fir branch about the eyrie.

The eaglets were growing fast. Their wing primaries were sprouting, and the feathers of the tail, shoulders, and back of the neck were showing. The tip and the base of each eaglet's bill was at this time black, and in the centre of the bill, near the nostril, was a curious yellow band. On the 30th of May my wife again took the early watch from 7.10 a.m. to 11 a.m. On her arrival the eaglets were asleep, and no signs of the old birds were seen on her way up. Doubtless they were still ranging the hills on their early morning hunt. The day was stormy with much wind and rain. At 10.10 a.m. the hen arrived. She had evidently come merely to see if the cock had returned home from his hunting, for after looking around she went off again. The eaglets did not seem to have noticed her arrival or departure, so they cannot have been hungry. At 10.40 a.m. there was a heavy rainstorm, and the eagle returned and stood in a crouching position to shelter the eaglets, but they only put their heads under her feathers, their white bodies remaining out in the rain. When the rain stopped she fed them both and then left.

She had probably heard my approach, for I arrived at the hide for my watch at noon soon after she had left. A few minutes after

I had entered the hide another drenching squall of sleet swept across the hill from the west. In twenty minutes the mother eagle alighted at the nest, and almost immediately after her arrival a fierce gust of wind blew a large piece of moss completely over my small peep-hole. Although I was most cautious in my efforts to remove the obstruction, the eagle must have become aware of some movement of the roof of the hide, for she left the nest. In twenty-five minutes she returned, and although at first she was suspicious, she commenced, after a few minutes, to feed Cain on a hare. She fed first one eaglet and then the other for an hour and five minutes, then brooded them in the rain that had commenced to fall. Cain was in a thoroughly bad mood to-day. When Abel cheeped for food she pecked out his down, and once pulled out a young growing feather from the body of her long-suffering brother. This feather stuck to her bill with great persistence, and caused her much inconvenience before she ultimately freed herself from it. Abel, with a most dejected expression, long awaited his turn to be fed, but when at last his mother condescended to take notice of him he "put away" an astonishing quantity of hare. A number of bones he swallowed whole, and even gulped down a large piece of the backbone. It was quaint to see him really gluttoning over his dinner.

The mother eagle was gentle and full of affection as she fed her son, and one looked in vain for her usual fierce and merciless expression. Despite her apparent indifference she really loved Abel. Once she was quite anxious during his desperate attempts to swallow a larger bone than usual, and seemed ready to snatch it from him if he showed signs of choking. She herself swallowed most of one leg and foot of the hare's carcase, and strained repeatedly at the leg before it disappeared down her throat.

At three o'clock she looked all round her expectantly, then walked majestically to the edge of the eyrie and stood apparently awaiting her mate. But he did not arrive, and at ten minutes past three she again fed the young birds for about twenty minutes, and then had a further meal herself.

At half-past three she brooded her young, for it was bitterly cold, with frequent squalls. At 3.50 p.m. she fell asleep, her head sunk forward, her eyes closed, her plumage matted and dripping with water. On her feathers beads of moisture stood; each splendid primary was visible, although the wings were folded in repose.

Thus she warmed her eaglets through a succession of storms, a figure of immense reserves of strength as she crouched low in her swaying eyrie and faced the squalls that rushed through the pines, while the gale made deep-toned music in the restless trees and stinging sleet harried the young growing things of the forest.

It must have been a cheerless and unprofitable business to hunt on such a day, for the time of the cock's arrival with food was by now four or five hours overdue, and still he came not.

At 6.15 p.m. I crawled from the hide, stiff, aching, and numbed by the cold.

I had reached the glen when I saw the cock pass low across a little wooded hill near me. Even as he flew, in the grey light I could recognise him by the very pale colour of his plumage. Although he had been hunting so long he was still without prey. He flew low, and perhaps a little wearily, against the wind, and I saw him stoop half-heartedly at a jackdaw which had crossed his line of flight.

My next watch in the hiding-tent was on 1st June, when I entered the hide at 8.50 a.m. A willow-warbler was daintily searching for insects at the edge of the eyrie, in which two grouse and part of a hare were lying. The eaglets were asleep, lying with their wings outstretched, and I noticed how rapidly the feathers of the back and wings had grown since my last visit. At 10.10 a.m. the father eagle flew in but stayed only one minute. Cain, as usual, realised his approach long before Abel. Twenty minutes after the parent had left the family, Cain commenced a very determined and entirely unprovoked attack upon her brother. She tore from his unfortunate person great billfuls of white down and even tiny feathers. Abel in desperation ran to the far side of the eyrie and lay there, quite still and very sullen. Cain thereupon stood up, flapped her downy wings, and uttered several wild and piercing yells of victory. There was an extraordinary and quite unearthly quality in these calls which deeply impressed itself upon my mind. Great billfuls of her brother's down adhered to her bill, and she had much trouble in ridding herself of the fruits of her easily gained victory.

At 11.20 a.m. the father eagle, who on his last visit had brought a rabbit to the eyrie, arrived with a grouse. He remained scarcely a minute, and this time neither eaglet noticed his arrival nor paid any attention to him. At 12 noon, after leaving my wife to take the afternoon watch, I saw the mother eagle soaring in the teeth of the breeze far above the hill-tops. She hung there like some aeroplane that has been brought almost to a standstill by a storm, or like some giant kite suspended aloft.

That afternoon the hen eagle did not return again to the eyrie; possibly the time was coming for the eaglets to learn to feed themselves, hence the growing infrequency of her visits. The cock, however, came again for the third time that day.

The following day, 2nd June, swifts were circling about the eyrie when I entered the hide just before noon. Beside the eagle's nest a cock redstart was perched, his fiery tail a-quiver. The eagles were beginning to bring grouse and ptarmigan unplucked to the nest (at an earlier stage every bird had been carefully plucked), and to-day a feathered grouse lay in the eyrie.

By this time I had learnt to expect the arrival of one of the parents when Cain commenced to yelp, but Abel called peevishly at all times and at the critical moment was usually silent. Thus when, at 12.30 p.m. Abel commenced to yelp I felt confident it was a false alarm, and sure enough no parent appeared. Perhaps because she was annoyed by her brother's stupidity, Cain shortly after this episode commenced to attack the long-suffering Abel, and tore clouds of down from him. While Cain paused for breath Abel sat perfectly still and silent, his head moodily sunk forward; after a time he collapsed at the bottom of the nest.

Just after two o'clock the eaglets called excitedly for some time. The mother eagle was possibly sitting on a neighbouring tree-top, but through my small peep-hole I could not see her. Fifteen minutes later the cock dropped in with a grouse, but, as usual, remained at the eyrie less than a minute. Almost immediately he had gone his mate sailed down to the nest from the west. She had probably been watching for his arrival from some neighbouring tree. She at once picked up a grouse that was lying in the eyrie and flew away with it held in one foot. A minute later, after a wide sweep round, she alighted with it at the nest, as though to make believe that she, and not the cock, had brought this food for the family!

Then ensued a painful scene. Cain, peevish on an empty crop, made a terrific onset upon poor Abel. It was by far the most determined attack I had yet seen, for she drove him mercilessly round and round the nest. The mother eagle, curiously enough,

THE FATHER EAGLE FEEDING THE EAGLET WITH TINY MORSELS OF FLESH.

paid not the least attention to the family row, but flew away and was absent for a few minutes. Possibly she thought they had better fight it out for themselves. During her mother's absence Cain behaved inexcusably. Her blood was up; undoubtedly she saw red. With wild cries of triumph she pursued Abel, pecking him brutally and pulling out his down so that it floated away on the breeze. Round and round the eyrie she chased her brother, raining blows on his "behind," his body, his head and neck. I had fears lest she should blind him, but he escaped that disaster. Abel in desperation once or twice retaliated very feebly, but when the mother eagle returned she found her son lying exhausted at the edge of the eyrie. She ignored his cheepings, and for a full half-hour fed his sister on grouse, giving her the flesh and the bones and bolting the entrails herself. It was only when Cain was gorged that she turned her attention to Abel, who, despite his severe beating, had a keen appetite! When she flew off after feeding him for a quarter of an hour he was quite indignant, for he was by no means satisfied. The eaglets were now in the fifth week of their lives.

Next day, 3rd June, my wife was in the hide from 12.25 p.m. to 2.45 p.m. On her arrival both eaglets were asleep. No food was to be seen in the eyrie. At 1 p.m. Abel commenced to preen his feathers, and it was noticed that the down on his thighs was a beautiful golden yellow. The little new black feathers showed clearly against the pure white of the down on his back and wings. At 2 p.m. the cock arrived with a rabbit and left at once, for the larder was almost bare, and he evidently thought hunting was an urgent necessity. In ten minutes the hen came and fed Abel first (for a wonder!) and then Cain. In twenty minutes she left, sailing out steadily into the breeze.

CHAPTER 4

A PAIR OF EAGLES AND THEIR HOME LIFE

For fifteen days we were unable to visit the eyrie, and when on 19th June I again climbed to it I found the eaglets had changed greatly during our absence.

Cain by now was well feathered all over; Abel's head was still white, and much white down remained upon his body. The eaglets were now about seven weeks old. The young birds had gradually changed in their behaviour to us. At first they had crouched motionless in the nest on our approach, but now regarded us with indifference.

Next day, 20th June, there was a fresh green pine branch and green bunches of heather lying in the eyrie, and on the heather a blue hare had been placed. The eaglets were peaceful that morning and from time to time stretched out their growing wings to their

32

full extent, holding them thus for some time.

At a quarter to one the cock eagle arrived with a grouse. He was a superb figure as he stood, very erect, on the edge of the eyrie, the midsummer sun shining full upon his light brown plumage. The family were so excited by his arrival that they almost pushed their father off the eyrie, and, hating to be hustled, he hastened his departure.

The eaglets were now able to tear up the prey for themselves, and Abel commenced to feed himself hungrily on the hare, Cain meanwhile lying "doggo."

Abel had developed wonderfully during the fifteen days we had been absent from the eyrie. No longer did he live in terror of Cain; they pecked at each other's bills amicably, and never from that time forward did we see them fight, nor Cain attack her brother.

At two o'clock that afternoon there was much yelping from Cain, who evidently spied one of the old birds pass overhead, and twenty minutes later the cock again arrived, holding in his claw what appeared to be the remains of a blackcock. Quickly he sailed away once more, and ten minutes later his mate arrived, but was scared off the eyrie by the sound of my focal plane shutter. Fifteen minutes later she returned, but she was still suspicious, and although I did not move she almost at once flew off. Ten minutes later she sailed in, this time carrying a bunch of heather in her bill. She laid it upon the eyrie, opened her wings and without effort sailed away. Within five minutes she was back again, picked up from the floor of the eyrie a small piece of meat, and carried it off.

This was a day full of thrills for the watcher. In five minutes the dark form of the mother eagle once more appeared for the fifth visit in two hours, during which time the cock had also come in twice. This time she carried in a pine branch for the decoration of the eyrie. She then rummaged carefully with her bill about the floor of the nest and ate small objects. On several occasions we saw her do this, and imagined she was eating the maggots from the ancient carcases lying about the eyrie.

All that afternoon the hen eagle came at short intervals to the eyrie, but was suspicious and did not feed the eaglets.

That day I left the hide shortly before six o'clock. As I commenced my walk down the hillside the cock eagle was sailing high overhead in a sky of deepest blue. He hung there like an aeroplane, the sun shining full upon his golden head so that it seemed almost white. Behind him rose great hills, still carrying wellnigh unbroken winter's snow upon their upper slopes. The north wind blew chill, and the whole countryside, after weeks of drought, was dry as tinder.

From the hide next day, 21st June, I saw how different was the weather east and west of me. Eastward dark clouds, bringing drizzling showers with them, drifted across the hills, but to the west was brilliant clear sunny weather, and upon Ben Nevis, Scotland's highest hill, the great snowfields gleamed.

Just after half-past one that day the cock eagle alighted at the eyrie bringing most unexpected prey to the eaglets – nothing less than a squirrel! Both eaglets were filled with excitement, calling loudly in unison. The different pitch in the voices of Cain and Abel was always interesting to hear. Abel's cheeping was shriller. His sister called in a lower key, and gave tongue less frequently but more strongly. At three o'clock that afternoon both eaglets seemed scared, as though danger approached. I feared that the noise might be caused by some intruders in this quiet part of the forest and that the eyrie might be discovered, but from my wee peep-hole I could not see anyone. Twice my wife had heard, on different occasions, the noise of human voices and the sound of nailed boots on the rocks below, but during the eleven weeks of our watching no person, as far as we know, discovered our eyrie and hiding-tent. During the afternoon first Abel, then Cain, fed heartily off a grouse, but left the squirrel alone.

On 23rd June my wife spent three hours in the afternoon at the eyrie. The parents were coming less often to the nest each day and were spending a shorter time on their visits. This day the hen came for a moment at 3.30 p.m., but did not attempt to help the eaglets in their feeding. The head-feathers of Cain were really golden now, and the rest of her plumage was a rich dark brown, but the white down was still showing on neck, breast, and shanks. Even Abel now had hardly any feathers on his head.

On 24th June my wife again took the watch for three hours in the morning, and this day was distinguished by the watcher seeing for the first time both eagles at the nest together. First the cock arrived, but Abel continued looking out and calling, and then the hen alighted, but only remained a minute. It was a magnificent picture to see all four birds at the eyrie at once. When the hen had gone the cock began to feed Cain on tiny pieces of meat. Like human fathers, he did not seem to realise that his family were no longer babies and could now tear off large pieces of flesh for themselves. Cain accepted rather scornfully the tender morsels which her parent gave her with the same great gentleness that he had used when his child was a chick in down. After a while Cain evidently thought she had sufficiently humoured her stupid father, and commenced to feed herself in a grown-up manner, whereupon the cock complacently fed himself!

In the eyrie were the foreleg and backbone of a roe-deer calf, and Cain sampled these, but gave them up in favour of a very old piece of grouse. Later on the two eaglets had a quarrel over a grouse, but after a tug of war Cain as usual proved her superior strength and wrested it from Abel. The call-note of the eaglets was still as childish as ever, but Cain was becoming more silent.

Next day, 26th June, was my watch, and at 10.30 a.m. I entered my observation post. Until 11.10 a.m. the eaglets lay quiet in the nest, then they commenced to preen themselves, and I noticed that they always closed their eyes when actually preening their feathers. When asleep they lay like dogs rather than birds, their heads pillowed on the eyrie. To-day another squirrel was in the nest. Its thick fur defeated Abel, and with rage he stamped upon it and dug viciously into it with his bill, carrying it about the eyrie in a comical fashion. After a time Cain took the squirrel from him and appeared about to attack poor Abel, who at once assumed an attitude of stoical dejection, remaining perfectly motionless as he awaited the expected onslaught, which, fortunately, did not materialise. Cain was more successful with the squirrel than her brother had been, for she succeeded in pulling out much of the resisting fur. She continued at her task perseveringly, and at length tore off and swallowed large pieces of the victim, which she bolted, fur and all!

Abel all this time was lying "doggo" in the eyrie. At 12.25 p.m. Cain made desperate efforts to swallow the squirrel whole, but was unsuccessful, and then, with unexpected pluck, Abel snatched it from her and commenced to eat it himself. I expected trouble between the eaglets, but Cain, although she looked amazed at this unlooked-for boldness, did nothing. Abel, after feeding awhile on the squirrel, also endeavoured to swallow it all, but even its now attenuated remains proved too much for him and he gave it up as a bad job.

At 1.30 p.m. the father eagle arrived and remained thirteen minutes at the eyrie, an unusually long time for him. First he fed himself, and had apparent repugnance in swallowing a quite small morsel of meat, perhaps too "high" even for his taste. He then attempted to feed Abel, who was now feeding himself stoutly. It was amusing to see him offer his large children dainty morsels, just as my wife had seen him do a few days previously. He seemed quite surprised when Abel (perhaps from a filial sense of duty) took them only after persuasion, or ignored his offerings entirely, so that his well-meaning father was obliged to eat them himself. How difficult it is for all fathers to believe that their children do in time grow up; even eagle fathers are no exceptions! One could almost hear the old eagle say to himself, "Bless me, these youngsters have grown up without my realising it!"

Cain during these attempts at feeding Abel cheeped mournfully, entirely neglected. At last the eagle spread his giant golden wings and sailed through the trees out of my view across the hill-face with magnificent grace. The eaglets were left alone, and I noticed that for the first time they fondled each other with their bills. Perhaps this was a sign that the battle between them was over at last. Later in the afternoon the cock eagle brought more food, over which, for the first time, flies were soon buzzing. Cain was engaged in hopping round and round the eyrie, flapping her wings as she did so; these were the first of the wing exercises we were to see so much of in later days. At 3.30 p.m. the hen arrived, but the eaglets continued cheeping, which showed me that the cock too must be near, but he did not come. At 4.15 p.m. that afternoon I was looking out for a moment through the opening of the hide when I saw what at first I took to be an insect against the sky. But in a second the supposed insect was seen to be the cock eagle, who swooped down from the hills at a truly incredible speed. In one foot he held a cock ptarmigan, unplucked. His meteoric arrival was the most wonderful thing I have ever seen in the bird world, and his descent was so swift that his impetus took him far beyond the eyrie, so that he had to sweep round and sail slowly in from

the opposite direction. A few minutes after he had laid the
ptarmigan on the eyrie and departed again, the hen came up to
the nest from the forest below with a branch in her bill. During
the next few minutes she left the eyrie three times, removing first
the ptarmigan, then some large object which I could not
distinguish, then another smaller object. She soared with each
carcase in turn along the hill-face, appearing curiously like an
airship with her burden gripped in one talon. I wondered whether
she might be removing the larder to some storehouse, as she soon
vanished from my sight, still soaring steadily. Possibly it was
intended as a lesson to the eaglets that food would not always be
brought to them at the eyrie, and she may have thought to herself
that father eagle was pampering these fast-growing youngsters
too much.

Abel at her last disappearance, seeing with alarm the rapidly
disappearing food supply, made haste during his mother's absence
to swallow entirely the squirrel's tail, fur and all! After this feat of
Abel's both eaglets played with the new fir branches in the eyrie.
At 5 p.m. the hen arrived with a stick. The eaglets continued calling,
and presently the cock alighted beside the hen, carrying in his bill
a bunch of heather. This was only the second time either of us had
seen both parent eagles together at the nest. The cock laid down
the heather, took wing, and presently returned with a second bunch,
so again I had the good fortune to see the two splendid eagles side
by side at the eyrie. The hen during this time had been feeding
herself, and now flew off, carrying with her the carcase of the
grouse which she had been eating. She quickly returned, and for
more than half an hour fed both young in turn, subsequently
gorging herself on the entrails of a fresh grouse. Towards the end
of their feed Cain and Abel were so replete that they could hardly
be induced to take the food she offered them.

The next watch was taken by my wife on 28 th June, commencing
at the early hour of 5.40 a.m. On the way up the hillside to the
eyrie she saw the cock eagle fly up and alight on a tree; perhaps he
had just returned from his early morning hunting. In the eyrie lay
one grouse, one ptarmigan, and an old piece of rabbit. Both eaglets
were calling, but no parent arrived and soon they slept. At 7 a.m.
both woke up and Cain did her early morning flapping exercises.
Then she slept again with her head under her wing. After a little

sleep she with difficulty threw up a large pellet, and seemed very surprised at this phenomenon. Both eaglets looked out anxiously for a sign of their parents. The day was still and warm, and the clouds of midges were bothering the eaglets as well as the silent watcher in the hide. The eaglets kept rubbing their heads and eyes against their necks and shoulders to knock off the midges. After a while Cain began to feed on the baby rabbit and managed to swallow a whole front leg, followed by the liver; then she had a second course of grouse. Cain was fast developing the build of the hen eagle. At this stage Abel, having completed a thorough toilet, also began to feed.

At 9.45 a.m. both eaglets became excited, and peered over the eyrie at the trees below them, calling loudly. My wife surmised that the parent bird was sitting on a tree below. After a while she heard the sounds of the great bird moving on a tree quite near, but her limited view from the peep-holes prevented her from seeing it. After quarter of an hour's expectation, shared by the anxious eaglets with my wife, she was privileged to see a wonderful sight. The cock eagle alighted, exhausted, at the eyrie with a roe-deer calf held in one great foot! The powerful bird arrived from below, and was only just able to raise himself to the nest with his large burden. Panting with the effort, he left the prey and stalked majestically across the eyrie, paying no attention to the wild shrieks of joy and excitement of his offspring. Like a happy child when brought a new toy Cain pounced on the roe calf with yells of triumph, similar to those she used after a successful attack on Abel, and tried to tear up the large "present." Abel vented his excitement by dashing up and down the eyrie with a feather in his bill. Both seemed hurt that father calmly fed himself on grouse! To make matters worse, the old eagle even offered his children pieces of old grouse, while all the time they were longing for a course of roe deer! Cain tried to lift the calf, and this gave my wife a chance to see it more clearly, and she was able to notice that it had had its head and entrails removed, no doubt to lighten it, for it must be remembered that the eagle brought this calf from the forest, certainly 500 feet below the eyrie. After twelve minutes the cock left the nest without having attempted to feed the eaglets or himself on the calf. For the remainder of the watch till 10.40 a.m. Cain remained standing on the calf, trying to tear it.

I took the afternoon watch on this day from 3.45 p.m. to 7 p.m. For the first time the house-flies were troublesome in the forest, and the biting horse-fly or "cleg" was abroad. This afternoon Cain and Abel were taken in completely by a gull soaring high over their eyrie; they fully believed it was one of their parents, and were thoroughly disgusted when it disappeared from view. The parent eagles did not visit the nest all afternoon. Next day, 29th June, my wife was in the hide from 10 a.m. to 3 p.m., but during this long watch, made all the more tedious by the swarm of flies, biting and otherwise, she only saw the hen bird alight once for a short visit to the eyrie.

CHAPTER 5

A PAIR OF EAGLES AND THEIR HOME LIFE

PREPARING FOR THE WIDE WORLD

A visit to the Hebrides kept us away from the eyrie until 3rd July. The eyrie was now swarming with flies, and in the nest were two more roe calves and the skeleton of the first. Cain was suffering severely from the swarms of house-flies, midges, and biting S*imulidae,* or sandflies. Every few seconds she rubbed her eyes against her shoulder, and often kept her eyes closed. The eyrie was no longer smart and tidy; it had become dirty and uncared for, with no fresh branches or heather. Cain could now walk about the eyrie with ease. Both birds slept off and on until 2.55 p.m. that day, when the cock alighted at the nest. Neither youngster showed pleasure at his coming, and he found the swarms of flies so unpleasant that he took wing in less than half a minute. It was becoming hard to distinguish Cain from

Abel, as both their heads were now feathered. The hen came rarely to the eyrie at this stage; to-day she did not appear once from noon till 5.45 p.m., when my watch ended.

The following day, 4th July, as I approached the hiding-tent at 9.10 a.m. both parent eagles were sailing high above me. Little remained of the roe-deer calves, and the parents as well as the eaglets must have been gorging on them. At 10.20 a.m. the cock came with a grouse, and for the next forty minutes Abel cheeped almost continuously. I imagined the hen was somewhere near, and was suspicious, as she may have seen me enter the hide. The cock several times brought prey to the eyrie this day, and I could see the fierce flash of his proud eye as, standing on the eyrie's edge, he scanned the glen below. On one visit he lifted in his bill the intestines of one of the roe-deer calves, but did not eat them; on another visit he had scarcely laid a grouse on the eyrie when Cain seized it in her talons and half flew with it across the eyrie. On the coming of a breeze, which momentarily drove off the crowd of flies, Abel flapped his wings excitedly, and I felt sure the eaglets might any day now take their first flight from the home that had given them shelter for close on ten weeks. Between 9 a.m. and 5 p.m. the cock paid five visits to the eyrie, usually carrying prey, but the hen never came to the nest.

The following day, 5th July, my wife took the watch from 10.40 a.m. to 3 p.m. The flies were increasing in multitude and vigour, and made life a burden to the eaglets and the inmate of the hide. She reported that the eyes of the eaglets seemed swollen by the attentions of the winged pests. The eaglets also suffered from the heat of the sun and panted much. The back of the neck and the breast of the eaglets were now the only parts that were not fully feathered, but Abel had not completely grown the new feathers on his thighs and rump. This was a day of sultry heat and thunder, and the eaglets seemed to be oppressed by the weather, for they slept most of the day. Neither parent bird came to the eyrie during the four and three-quarter hours of watching. The 6th July proved equally uneventful. The eaglets were standing in the eyrie when my wife arrived at the hide at 10.40 a.m., and did not bother to crouch down in the nest, for by now they had come to regard us as a nuisance rather than a danger. The eyrie daily became more flattened and sloping at the edges. Once or twice the parent birds evidently passed over but never came to the nest. It seemed clear that they had begun to encourage the young to leave the eyrie by the infrequency of their visits and the rationing of the eaglets.

Next day, 7th July, I again took the watch, and this was a red-letter day from the observer's point of view, for Cain fell from the eyrie owing to the part of it on which she was standing giving way beneath her. With her fell a whole roe calf and a grouse! From my hiding-place I did not see the actual fall, for it took place on the side farthest away from me, but to my astonishment I saw Cain, who had seemed safe in the nest a few minutes before, walking along the ground, looking scared and wild, away from the eyrie. She soon disappeared from my sight, and I did not again see her. Abel was from now onward alone in the eyrie.

The parent eagles were evidently putting their young on short rations in order to induce them to leave the nest. At 12.45 p.m. the cock arrived with a plucked bird of some kind, and this proved to be almost the last time either of us saw him at the eyrie. Abel instantly seized the prey from him but did not attempt to feed on it. At 2.15 p.m. the hen appeared. She carried an unplucked cock grouse, which Abel seized from her.

At 2.20 p.m. the cock brought a rabbit. Cain after his departure seized a grouse in one foot and the plucked bird in the other, and tried to walk across the eyrie with them, but failed. He then lay on his side with one wing outstretched, and one leg stuck out to its fullest extent, just like a dog. Both eaglets at this stage made periodic rushes across the eyrie, evidently practising "taking off" in preparation for their first flight.

When Cain fell out of the nest Abel was asleep, and did not realise for some time that he was alone.

On 8th July (the next day) my wife spent five hours in the hide, and during this day witnessed the last call at the eyrie of the hen bird, who, however, remained only a few seconds.

The remnants of yesterday's rabbit and unplucked cock grouse were all that were now left at the eyrie for Abel's sustenance, and no fresh prey was brought. The day was passed by Abel in much wing-flapping and hopping and clutching exercises, alternating with sleep and preening to rid himself of the remains of his down. Several times the parent eagles circled over the eyrie, causing Abel

THE COCK EAGLE LIVING UP TO HIS AGE-OLD REPUTATION OF BEING THE
KING OF BIRDS.

to call piteously, but with no avail. They were most certainly trying to encourage him to leave the eyrie and join his sister.

On 9th July I took my turn again, and during the day's watch saw Abel sleeping in the orthodox bird fashion with his head under his wing, the only time I had seen him do this. At 1.30 p.m. he had a fair meal of grouse, eating all there was left of it except some of the small intestines. The rectum or large intestine he ate, as a titbit perhaps, at the very end of his meal. Several times he tried unsuccessfully to hold the gizzard with his feet, and at last got a grip of it and soon polished it off. After his repast he indulged in vigorous wing exercises, giving great hops as he flapped his wings violently. To-day for the first time no parents appeared at the eyrie, and I noticed that they were no longer removing the carcases, so that the nest was untidy and evil-smelling.

Next day, 10th July, I again had a long watch, always hoping to see Abel's first flight. The remains of two half-plucked ptarmigan were in the eyrie, so these must have been brought in the early morning or the night before. Abel dozed happily till 10.45 a.m., when a wren in full song just beside the eyrie gave him a surprise. Ten minutes later he called loudly. One of the parents evidently passed overhead, but, to Abel's annoyance, did not come near him. At 11.30 a.m. he again gave tongue, and with his eyes followed the line of his parent's flight. Again he was disappointed, and now with outspread wings leapt fiercely on one of the ptarmigan and commenced to devour it. This ended, he began to practise a curious grabbing exercise He made sudden fierce snatches at the old remains of the roe calves, looking extremely wild as he shot out his strong talons. A "course" of flapping exercises followed, and he practised so strenuously that he almost flew out of the eyrie by mistake. By midday he had left nothing of the ptarmigan except the bone; he had even swallowed the entrails. He was reduced to playing with sticks in the eyrie, and subsequently slept until 2.15 p.m., when further jumping, snatching, and wing exercises filled up the afternoon. I was interested to see a single swift hawking flies above the eyrie; several times recently I had seen it there.

The 11th July was a brilliant summer day. On reaching the eyrie I made sure that Abel had flown, for at first I could not see him anywhere. Then I saw him at the extreme lower edge of the eyrie, almost hidden by a small branch. There was nothing but one small rabbit in the nest. At noon Abel made a meal of this rabbit, and now the cupboard was bare. After this meal he peered down over the eyrie eagerly, as if wondering if he dare penetrate to the big world around and below him, and then he began to play with the swaying fir branches, pecking at them but usually missing them. Later I was interested to see that he stood in the eyrie with one of his feet tightly closed and resting on the nest. Subsequently he lay for a time with his tail pointing straight upwards. No more prey was brought to the eyrie during my watch; the parents had seriously commenced to starve poor Abel to induce him to leave the nest. It was evident that Abel was now increasingly tormented by biting flies. Besides the ubiquitous midge, the eyrie swarmed with small speckled *Simulidae*. The bite of these small flies is very poisonous, and after a single bite from one of them my whole leg swelled up. So poor Abel, constantly bitten about the eyes by swarms of these insects, was much to be pitied. On leaving the hide I paid a visit to the unoccupied eyrie of the same pair of eagles a few miles away. There were new breast-feathers in it, showing that the parent eagles must have used it sometimes – perhaps to roost in. "Castings" of the parent eagles lay near this eyrie. The golden eagle ejects the fur and bones of its prey in the form of a pellet, and these pellets are sometimes remarkably large. One which I measured was three inches long and five inches in circumference. On a knoll near the eyrie was the fur of many blue hares, and it was evidently here that most of the prey was plucked.

On 12th July my wife was in the hide most of the day but saw nothing more of the parents, and Abel continued his lonely and rather hungry routine of life. On 13th July, quite without intention, I nearly caused Abel's premature departure from the eyrie. Seeing him nowhere about on my arrival at the hide, and seeing also that the eyrie was bare of food, I made sure he had at last taken his first flight, and so (with difficulty) I climbed to the eyrie. As I peered over the top of the nest I had the fright of my life, for Abel suddenly flapped his great wings at me with fury! I feared he would fly off, but he did not do so.

From the eyrie to-day was a glorious prospect. On Ben Alder the sun shone full upon the lingering snowfields. The lower slopes of Ben Nevis were hidden in a dense white cloud, above which the higher reaches and summit of the mountain showed clear. The hot sun was drawing from the pines their delightful scent. The rainless weather had continued for so long that on the dry banks the blaeberry plants were withered and dead, and even the heather was scorched and brown. I crept into the hide, being followed by a great swarm of house-flies and not a few clegs; but luckily these insects rarely entered the hiding tent, although the midge and the house-flies made their presence felt even there. After a time Abel, recovering from his fright, flew up from his branch to the crown of the eyrie and commenced fierce grabbing exercises. Doubtless hunger had made him fiercer, for he evidently had had little, if any, food for two days, and was ravenous. His exercises finished, he lay on the eyrie panting in the heat, and looking everywhere for his parents. During these last days of his stay in the nest it was quite distressing to see his hunger. But he was being brought up in a hard school, and although he must have suffered from thirst even more than hunger, one could do nothing for him. (Although eaglets never drink during their three months' stay at the eyrie, they receive all the liquid necessary in the blood of the prey which they devour.) At 3 p.m. he made quite a good flight across the eyrie, and then hopped about, holding in one foot the ancient remains of a dried-up rabbit, useless for food even in his famished condition. He pathetically tried to eat one after the other of the dried-up carcases, but spat them out, finding them impossible to swallow. He then hopped down to his perch of the morning, where he was invisible to me in the hide. At 4 p.m. he sprang back into the nest without difficulty and at once commenced a new search for food. When he realised that the eyrie contained nothing to eat, furiously he gripped the carcase of a roe calf, making fierce grabs at it with his talons and then carrying it about. More vigorous wing exercises followed, and when I left him at 5.35 p.m. he was moodily scanning the skies for his neglectful parents, the picture of misery.

On 15th July my wife took the day's watch in the hide. Abel was still there, half starved, and with scarce the strength to call for his callous father and mother. Again the eyrie was empty of food, and the eagles never came near it all day. At last, on 16th July, after being alone in the nest nine days, the eaglet took wing and left the eyrie which had been his home for eleven weeks. Hunger drove him forth, and spreading his great wings, he mounted unsteadily into the air on the arms of the breeze, and disappeared for ever from our view.

As we dismantled the hide that had concealed us for nearly one hundred and seventy hours during the three months of the eagles' nesting, the sky darkened and quickly two thunderstorms formed, one north of us and the other south. Against the inky clouds blinding flashes of lightning followed each other in rapid succession. In torrents the rain descended, refreshing the parched hillside with its trees, heather, and many alpine plants. We pictured the eaglet, perhaps by now with his sister, fiercely gazing at the approaching storm from the topmost branches of some ancient gnarled pine far up on the hillside. Although he had left the nest he had still to be taught how to capture the blue hare and the swift-flying ptarmigan. For two months or longer he and his sister would remain with the parent eagles, often sailing above the hill-tops in the glow of the summer sun, often sheltering from gales and storms in some rocky recess, or steering unflinchingly into an autumn blizzard of stinging sleet.

But at length would come a day when the same parents who had so carefully tended them during their youthful months would turn upon their children with ferocity and drive them forth into the wide world to make a home for themselves on new territory.

CHAPTER 6

A PAIR OF EAGLES AND THEIR HOME LIFE

Conclusions

Altogether thirty-one days, spread over a period of eleven weeks, and a total of one hundred and sixty-seven hours, were spent at the eyrie described in the last four chapters, and from the observations made during this time, and at other eyries watched either before that season or subsequent to it, the following conclusions are based.

It is easy to cause a golden eagle to desert her nest if she be disturbed too frequently *before* the eggs are hatched, but she rarely forsakes the *eaglets* – indeed I doubt much whether she would ever do so unless actually shot at.

The eagle is a close sitter during the five weeks she is hatching her eggs. After the family are hatched she is more wary and leaves the eyrie while the human intruder is still a considerable distance away.

She does not brood them after the first fortnight even if the wind be cold so long as it is dry, but shelters them from rain or sleet.

In a tree-eyrie the eaglets are safe, but in an accessible rock eyrie they are at the mercy of any prowling fox. It would be interesting to know whether a fox has ever eaten an eaglet during its early downy stages. My own opinion is that Reynard holds the old eagles in too much respect to incur their wrath by venturing very near an eyrie. There is no other foe the eagle has to fear if man be excepted – and it is perhaps because she has not as yet fully learned by the experiences of successive generations the hostility of man that the eagle so often makes her eyrie on small rocks where it can be reached without difficulty.

The eaglets pass through three stages in the eyrie. During the first stage they are clothed in very thick white down; this stage lasts for four weeks. The second stage may be termed the black-and-white stage, when the feathers are beginning to sprout; this stage lasts about four weeks. The third, or feathering stage proper, lasts about three weeks. The last part of the bird to be feathered is the back of the head.

From the first there is no doubt about the sex of the eaglets. When two eggs are hatched, one *always* produces a cock, the *other always* produces a hen. The hen from the day of hatching is the larger and stronger of the two, and I have no doubt that the young hen frequently kills her brother. (It would be interesting to know whether this mortality among cock eaglets results in a preponderance of female adult eagles, or whether the sexes are made even again by hens being more frequently caught in traps or shot.)

The eaglets are dependent upon their parents for the tearing up and plucking of their food for at least a month; they gradually learn to tear up the carcases for themselves, and at last the prey is merely left in the eyrie. When the eaglets are very young the gentleness of the mother bird is astonishing. She pulls tiny pieces off grouse, ptarmigan, hare, or rabbit and holds them out to the eaglet she is feeding in an extraordinarily gentle and careful manner. Indeed, she shows her mother-love much more than many other birds, such as the raven and the grey crow; more, even, than the blackbird and thrush, who often seem rough in their feeding methods.

In the eyrie which my wife and I had under such close observation the hen never, or scarcely ever, hunted, but she did almost all the feeding. It was extraordinary how rarely both parent eagles were at the nest together. From some tree near the hen watched for the cock's return, and then, within a minute or so of his coming to the eyrie and depositing the food there, flew down on to the nest to feed the eaglets on the food just brought by the cock. The only regular meal which we noticed was the afternoon one.

From seven weeks onwards the eaglets practise wing exercises, and towards the end of their time in the nest they frequently practise grabbing exercises.

There is no doubt that if the old birds consider that either of the young eagles is dilatory in leaving the eyrie they force it by starvation to take its first flight.

The eyrie takes at least six weeks in the building or the repairing, and the eagles continue to bring fresh fir branches and bunches of heather to the eyrie until the last fortnight before the nest is vacated – that is, until the eaglets are about nine weeks old.

The golden eagle has no special likes or dislikes in the matter of diet. It is fond of grouse and ptarmigan, but prefers the blue or mountain hare to either of these birds. One eyrie near my own home in Inverness-shire is situated on the fringe of a grouse moor, where the mountain hare is numerous, and here the eaglets are fed almost entirely upon hares although grouse are plentiful.

It is remarkable that almost every writer of earlier days – and by this I mean books published so recently as the middle of last century – makes mention of the fact that the eagle will not hesitate to attack anyone venturing near its eyrie. If we accept these stories – and it would, I think, be unfair to doubt them all – we are driven to the conclusion that the habits of the golden eagle have changed and, perhaps from bitter experience, it has recently become much more wary and aloof. I have never heard of a golden eagle venturing to attack anyone at its eyrie. Frequently I have stood at a nest and seen the eagle perched on some rock on the hill-top on the farther side of the glen. Although I have handled her eaglets she has never shown any signs of agitation, let alone a desire to attack me; and personally I have only once known an eagle fly anywhere near the eyrie when it has been visited, and that bird flew over once or twice rather nervously. (Just as the book is going to press I have heard of an eagle attacking two persons photographing her eaglets in a western deer forest. The eagle passed so close in her rush that, in the words of my informant, "the noise of her wings sounded like the roar of a shell.")

There is an interesting peculiarity of the eagle that I have not seen mentioned, and that is its habit of leaving the eyrie in complete silence. The buzzard mews repeatedly on leaving her nest, and the peregrine falcon shrieks incessantly. But I have only once known an eagle who habitually called, with her curious far-carrying yelp, on leaving her eggs. Perhaps that particular bird had some prophetic instinct that her home would meet with disaster, for when the eggs were near hatching the stalker on whose beat the eyrie was built, lighted a large heather fire in the forest to burn the old heather. The eyrie was on a small rock on a steep hillside. The heather was very dry, and the flames crept up a small heather-clad gully, reached the eyrie, and set fire to it. When I visited it the next day I found the great pile of sticks still smouldering and the two eggs thoroughly baked.

There is, I think, no doubt that the downward rush of the golden eagle is the swiftest thing, as it is the most magnificent thing, in the bird world. The downward stoop of the peregrine is generally given pride of place, but it must be remembered that the peregrine is very small compared with the eagle, and that a small bird always seems to be travelling faster than a large one; for example, a blackcock looks to be flying slower than a red grouse, yet is moving considerably faster. Even the usual effortless flight of the eagle is inspiring to watch; its downward rush is a thing of magnificent power and a joy for ever.

Once the eaglets take their first flight from the eyrie it is difficult to follow them. If the young are reared in a pine forest they remain in the vicinity of the nest for nearly a week. They perch on the topmost branches of some fir tree, and there await the coming of their parents with food. Sometimes they are pestered by grey crows, and I have seen a young eagle driven ignominiously into the depths of a wood by the persistent attacks of a number of these impudent birds.

In August, and in the first part of September, young and old eagles are together, and the parents are teaching the eaglets how to hunt. It is mid-September when the eaglets leave their parents. It is not known, I think, whether they are driven off by the old birds or whether they sail out into the wide world of their own accord, but late in September or early in October I have often seen a solitary eaglet hunting. What becomes of the young eagles? They do not nest until they are four years old, and yet almost all the eagles seen in the spring are nesting, and therefore mature birds. It is possible that the young migrate, and it seems likely that the flock of nine eagles seen in September recently – and mentioned in another chapter – were young birds of the year on a journey, perhaps overseas.

Many of my correspondents confirm my own experience that one eaglet attacks the other. Although they have never actually seen this happen, they have seen one eaglet disappear and have sometimes found it dead on the ground below the eyrie.

One stalker tells me that he found both eaglets dead on the rocks below the nest, and I imagine that this fight must have been an unusually fierce and evenly matched one, and that both eaglets lost their balance during the battle.

A stalker who has throughout his life made observations on the eagle tells me that in the eighty-two eyries he has seen occupied in the course of his time – he has kept a careful diary – there were eight clutches of three eggs, fifteen clutches of one egg only, and two eggs in all the remaining nests. I have heard from another reliable source of the finding of four eggs in an eagle's nest, rather below the normal size, however. The Duke of Argyll tells me that he once knew of a pair of eagles rearing three young; but this must have been exceptional, for in all the eight clutches of three eggs mentioned above, never more than two eaglets were hatched. A stalker, who is a keen naturalist, tells me that he has seen eagles tearing up the heath-rush (I presume this would be *Luzula sylvatica*) in October and November and collecting it in March for the lining of the nest.

The same stalker writes: "The eagle usually sits on the nest thirty days. [This is five days less than the generally accepted incubation period.] Sometimes there are four days between the laying of the first and the second egg, but she sits on the nest as soon as the first egg is laid. I have seen a newly hatched eaglet as late as 20th June." This would seem to point to the eagle laying a

Leaving the eyrie. This picture shows the enormous wing-spread of
the golden eagle.

second time occasionally, but from all accounts it is quite exceptional.

Elsewhere I have mentioned that the eagle usually occupies the same eyrie every second year, but a stalker, who knows of a number of nests, tells me there is one eyrie which has been used for six seasons in succession. Another correspondent mentions that a pair of eagles had their nest three years in succession on the extreme top of a fir tree.

I close this chapter with a list of prey found by myself or my correspondents either at eagles' eyries, or found newly killed with the eagle beside them.

Four-footed Animals	*Birds*
Mole	Bird's egg[1]
Stoat	Golden plover
Weasel	Lapwing
Black water-vole	Blackcock
Fox cub	Greyhen
Domestic cat	Red grouse
Small collie dog	Ptarmigan
Lamb	Domestic fowl
Young goat	Magpie
Hare	Raven
Rabbit	Grey crow
Squirrel	Rook
Rat	Jackdaw
Roe-deer fawn	Heron
Red-deer fawn	Sea-gull

Fish

Salmon	Pike

[1] Probably this came from the oviduct of a bird that had been taken to the eyrie.

An eagle takes off from its perch.

CHAPTER 7

THE COUNTRY OF THE EAGLE

EARLY SPRING IN THE CAIRNGORMS

"The eagle, he was lord above,
And Rob was lord below" – Wordsworth.

In the forest of old pines the March sun shone with power upon the sunny knolls where blackcock warmed themselves after the tourney of the dawn. There was shelter in the forest, but higher up the glen the air was keen and frosty and the ground powdered with snow. At a height of 1500 feet above the sea the winter snows were almost unbroken; the overnight fall lay lightly upon them. The track here followed a hill stream with waters so clear that every stone could be seen in the deeper pools. Even thus high, 1600 feet above the level of the sea and a full seventy miles from the coast, do salmon come at the season of their spawning, and the hill otter follows them and takes heavy toll of the far-traveled and weary company.

The young river today was fringed with a snow wall from 6 to 10 feet in height, blindingly white in the strong spring sunshine. It was curious to see a water-ousel or dipper standing upon this Arctic wall, his glossy black plumage in striking contrast to the surrounding snows.

Although winter still lingered in this upland glen the grouse were pairing, so that there was much animation among the "heather cocks" this morning and rivalry over the claiming of nesting territory. For some time two old cock grouse flew excitedly backwards and forwards, the pursuer never allowing the pursued to rest until they both alighted for breath upon the short heather.

In February a fierce southerly gale had swept the glen. It had piled the soft powdery snows high in sheltered hollows, and in one place the track was buried beneath fully 20 feet of snow, so firmly packed that one could walk on its surface without sinking in an inch.

At the head of the glen is a lonely hill loch. From it the cliffs rise sheer to a height of almost 4000 feet, and in these black rocks the golden eagle has her eyrie. I knew the eagle was at home today because of the behaviour of the grouse. They flew high overhead, moving this way and that, and seeming very unsettled and worried. Soon the eagle flew silently past, following closely the contour of the hill and sailing only a few feet above the ground. The great feather-clad legs were held outstretched towards the ground, in order, no doubt, that the eagle might grasp the more readily any luckless grouse or hare that might suddenly come in the field of her keen vision. I passed beneath the eyrie, but as yet there was no sign that the eagle had commenced to repair her home.

The hill loch today resembled some sheet of water of the Arctic. At the north end of the loch, where the waters are shallow, much ice was stranded. Here and there from the frozen shallows large rounded heaps of ice rose. They were shaped like ant-hills, and were of unusual and arresting appearance. They had apparently been formed by the showers of spray which a southerly gale had continuously thrown over some stranded ice-floes. Immediately it touched them the spray had frozen, so that an ever-thickening icy covering had grown up around the floes.

Along the margin of the loch I made my way. Near the farther
shore a goosander drake drifted like a small iceberg upon the water.
Deep, unbroken snow extended to the water's edge. The wild sheep
which have now lived on these hills for a decade (they escaped
being "gathered" when the hills were under sheep during the years
of the War) were tamed by hunger. They had been scraping for
food near the water, and it was a tribute to their vigour that they
had survived the snowfall which had covered the hills for a full
eight weeks.

In the corrie above the loch a couple of cock ptarmigan were
pursuing each other on snowy wings, for even thus high spring
was stirring the pulses of living things. But soon the sun was
obscured, and from the north a menacing squall of snow drifted
quickly up the glen and soon reached the loch. Before its coming
the air had been calm and the loch unruffled, but as the squall
reached the loch a dark line showed on the margin of the hill waters
as the icy wind current stirred them. Swiftly the breeze passed
along the loch, and from the grim precipices the snow was caught
up in powdery clouds that seemed black against the darkening
skyline high above the loch. Across the cliffs the Polar wind made
stern music; the corries were hidden in drifting snow. Soon the
farther shore of the loch was invisible, and the snow and hail,
scarcely melting in the icy water, floated on the surface in long
grey lines as though they were foam whipped up by the wind.

Against the ice-barrier, which projected almost everywhere from
the snowy slopes a few yards into the water, the spray from
momentarily increasing waves spouted high. Ever more fiercely
did the wind blow, and in the gathering gloom the grey snow was
drifted past in ghostly clouds.

When, for a minute, the storm lessened I saw the eagle perched
upon the hill-top opposite. On a knife-like ridge the great bird
stood, seemingly indifferent to the bitter wind, then, as I watched,
she (it was the hen bird) sprang magnificently into space and
mounted on her broad wings on the frosty breeze. Always upon
that narrow aerial ridge the eagle stands: in winter when all the
hills sleep below their soft covering of snow; in summer when at
noon the deer in the grassy corrie below drowse in the warm
stillness. Here, from her lofty perch, the eagle can see hill, loch,
and corrie, and westward, peak upon peak merging, in the far,

dream-like distance, in the last mountain outposts that guard the approaches to Tir nan Og. Does her mind ponder upon those vast distances, great even for her with her unrivalled flight? Or does she watch rather for the swift-wheeling ptarmigan that drift in a white-winged clan across the loch far below; or the mountain hares that play upon the hill-face where the heather is not too long; or perhaps the golden plover that speed past on arrow-swift flight calling for the things that have gone away upon the breeze of the hills and will return no more?

But there is one object that her keen eye is ever eager to see, and that is the dark form of her mate – for the golden eagle pairs for life, and is as constant in her affections as she is stern and bold in her nature. How wonderful it is when her mate appears to see the two mount up on dark pinions! Up, and ever up, the two rise, sailing together far above the topmost peaks and entering the country of the winds and the soft, drifting clouds, where they fly at such an immense height that they are invisible to the eye.

I remember one mid-December day climbing the corrie where the eagle has her perch. The winter wind was striking the dark loch in its deep cradle in fierce gusts, now from one quarter, now from another, and lifting the water in grey clouds of spindrift. In the corrie there were fierce squalls that drove the snow in whirling clouds high above the hill-top. These clouds seemed like the spray from some waterfall that is caught up from Hebrid cliffs when an Atlantic gale roars by to the sound of the deep music of breaking seas. Sometimes the drifting snow was so dense that it was almost impossible to breathe; a few seconds later a great stillness would settle over the snowy expanse. Suddenly a small covey of ptarmigan flew past and alighted on the snow; others followed them, flying excitedly, and I knew that the eagle was abroad. Soon the hunter came into view. He was flying at a great height above the loch. Now he rose almost vertically into the air; now, closing his great wings, he stooped earthward like a plummet. He passed over, heedless of the ptarmigan, and these hill-dwellers commenced to feed upon the shoots of the crowberry on an exposed ridge where the snow scarcely lay. In my diary for that date I find I have written: "Yesterday I heard the wild swans of snowy plumage call deep-toned from their ice-fringed loch. Today, amid the drifting snows, I saw the eagle of dark plumage hunting the snow-white clan of the ptarmigan, and exulting in the splendid strength of his flight." Wild swan and ptarmigan – what birds have more snowy plumage than these? Even the sea-gull is sombre and grey in comparison with them.

Twice more, that short winter's day, the eagles passed me. Once I saw a single ptarmigan cross over at a great height. He was swaying and rocking in his flight – a sure sign that the eagle had disturbed him – and was travelling with the wind at great speed. For a second or two he was in sight, then like a whirling snowflake he was gone beyond the powdery drift on the hill-crest. Looking in the direction whence he had come I saw the cock eagle a full mile distant. Across a great precipice he flew, and I made sure he had alighted on one of its ledges, but a short time afterwards he mounted above the ridge and continued his upward flight until he was invisible in drifting clouds. It was towards sunset when his mate passed me. In the glen below there were many wonderful lights. Opal-tinted the loch lay. It was the home of small-crested waves – for the wind had lessened and fierce squalls no longer played upon the waters.

From beside the waves rose steel-blue snowy slopes; far below in the valley the setting sun burned upon russet bracken and brown moorland. The hen eagle passed close to me. She was fighting with the uncertain wind currents, which were tossing even her like a small boat in a choppy sea, but as she stood out from the hill she felt the steady breeze, and sailed in serene spirals higher and ever higher.

Soon the sun had set, and the moon, full orbed, rose golden above the snowy slopes to shine upon dark loch and frozen corrie, and I pictured the eagle gripping tightly her cold perch of rock on the great precipices where the winter's snow can find no lodgment.

Perhaps, on this March day of drifting snow and increasing bitter wind, the eagle had left her perch to seek a more sheltered ledge – for the storm was now sweeping furiously up the glen, and it was across a dreary country that I fought my way to the lower ground along the farther shore of the hill loch. Here and there great snow "slides " extended into the loch, so that I was forced to wade out into the icy waters to avoid them. At times, too, I fell waist-deep into the snow amongst boulders as the thin, treacherous snow-crust broke beneath my weight. But late that afternoon, when at length I reached the fringe of the forest and heard the vibrating song of a lonely curlew above the snow-covered pines, the sunshine that had succeeded the snow spoke of spring that was surely at hand, despite the icy hand of Cailleach Bheur, the age-old spirit of winter.

CHAPTER 8

THE COUNTRY OF THE EAGLE

APRIL ON THE ROOF OF SCOTLAND

"Eagles may seem to sleep wing-wide upon the air" – KEATS.

In the sheltered glens April is a season of spring-tide. In the budding trees the stormcock sings, the lapwing wheels in mad courtship flight, and the first summer migrants, the ring-ousel and wheatear, are seen. But on the high Cairngorms April is often the most rigorous month of the year. For weeks the temperature may continue below the freezing-point, and fresh snow may be added almost daily to the many successive winter falls that lie unthawed in the high corries.

In Glen Eanaich, this day of which I write, the snowline was reached at 1400 feet, and beside the burn a great snowdrift, certainly 20 feet deep, lay across the road. A pair of cheery water-ousels were courting here, and all at once I saw grouse pass in an unending stream at great speed down the glen. There must have been at least two hundred of these alarmed birds, and from their behaviour I knew the eagle must be hunting near. Soon the eagle came into sight. She – from her great size it was evident the bird was a hen – soared leisurely north, following the same line as the fleeing birds but making no effort to overtake them.

In Coire Beanaidh the snow lay deep. Even the swift burn flowed continuously beneath the snow. In the corrie were no grouse, no ptarmigan even; the snowy acres were lifeless as a Polar expanse. There was no breeze; and the strong sun was thawing the snow and causing small snowballs to roll down from the ice-encrusted rocks at the head of the corrie. Two feet of fresh snow lay on the earlier falls. This new snow was soft and sticky so that each step was an effort, but the glorious view was a constant joy, and by noon I had reached the head of the corrie and looked westward across to the black precipice of Sgoran Dubh, each narrow ledge of which was dazzlingly white in the strong spring sunshine.

Near the head of Coire Beanaidh a little knoll was almost free of snow. Here the footmarks of a ptarmigan showed. I could see that the bird had alighted on the snow beside the knoll and had partaken of a frugal meal, picking off the young shoots of the heather that showed above the snow. But there was scarcely a bare knoll in all Coire Beanaidh today, and so the ptarmigan had been driven elsewhere to obtain even their Spartan diet.

At the head of the corrie one climbs steeply, to emerge on the ridge which forms the "march" between the deer forests of Rothiemurchus and Mar. The snowy surface here was icy and treacherous; it had been partially thawed, then frozen again. So smooth and glassy was this surface that the recent snows had found no resting-place upon it, but had been swept by the wind into the corrie below.

From the ridge I looked south over a snowy wilderness to the slopes of Ben MacDhui. On all that great hill no single speck of black showed, and beyond it eastward rose other snowy peaks- Beinn Mheadhon, Beinn A'an, Beinn a' Bhuird, and Cairngorm itself.

The sky was of a deeper blue than I could have believed possible, and behind the snowy crest of Sron na Lairige the heavens appeared almost black although they were cloudless.

SWALLOWING A BLUE HARE'S LEG, WHICH IS TOO BIG FOR THE EAGLETS.

There was little snow on the ridge, but each boulder was encased in feathery fog crystals, which grew out from the stones on which they had been formed by a mist-laden northerly wind.

From the ridge of Coire Beanaidh to the summit of Brae Riach is a climb of not more than three hundred feet.

On the hill-top, 4248 feet above sea-level, the scene was inconceivably grand and awe-inspiring. Not even in Spitsbergen had I seen an expanse of country so truly Arctic. It was entirely lifeless, and the pleasant glens far below seemed to belong to a different country, even to a different age. There is a cairn of stones marking the summit of Brae Riach. This cairn is perhaps five feet in height and is a prominent landmark, but today I looked in vain for it, and gradually came to realise that it was buried so deep in the snow that there was nothing to show where it stood. Thus the snow on the hill-top must have averaged at least six feet in depth, probably much more.

A few feet south of the cairn is the great precipice that drops to Coire Bhrochain. Even in summer, on a day of mist and strong wind, it is not safe to venture too near this precipice; today a cornice of snow was suspended over its edge, and it was impossible to know whether I was walking with solid ground a few feet below me or over an invisible abyss of a full thousand feet.

Across the white slopes of the Garbh Choire, Cairntoul rose. Its snowy cone caught the sunlight; in its high corrie Lochan Uaine (the Green Loch) was entirely hidden beneath ice and snow. Once when a cloud drifted up from the west the air immediately became bitterly cold, and a little below me a whirling cloud of snow was caught up on an eddy of wind. Even in the strong sunshine of a perfect spring day there was an almost menacing lifelessness in the prospect from this wild hill-top.

In the fury of a blizzard, when grey mists mingle with the hurrying snows, no human being could long survive the cold at these heights; he would share the fate of the migrating robin which I once found dead on the snow on the Cairngorms at a height of 3000 feet above sea-level. Blizzards sweep the dark precipices of the high Cairngorms even in May, and so the golden eagle does not build her eyrie on the precipices of Coire Bhrochain or the cliffs of Cairntoul. The eagle nests early, at a time when the ledges of these precipices are deep in snow, and even if they were clear an eyrie built upon them might be drifted up by a fresh snowstorm at any time.

But today fine weather prevailed across Scotland as far as sight could reach. Ben Nevis, fifty miles to the west, was in clear sunshine; north of that hill many white peaks rose from beside the distant Atlantic. To the north Ben Wyvis rose; below its snowy slopes the blue waters of the Moray Firth lay. Southward, far below me, the track of the Lairig led through the heart of the Cairngorms to where the blue smoke of the clachan at Inverey rose into the clear air.

Westward from the summit of Brae Riach a plateau extends for fully a mile and a half. As I crossed this plateau no single stone or rock showed through the deep uniform coat of snow that covered this, the highest plateau in all Scotland. The headsprings of the river Dee are here, but were buried beneath many feet, perhaps many yards, of snow, and the young river flowed entirely beneath the snow across the plateau.

West of the precipices that drop to Coire an Lochain I commenced the descent to Glen Eanaich by a slope so steep and icy that walking was not easy. A slight breeze from the west had begun to blow. Drifting at once commenced. Over the icy surface the powdery snow crept in small waves that reminded me of the inflowing tide on a low, sandy shore. With the breeze came dark clouds that drifted up from the south-west, but the sun flooded Coire an Lochain and its loch. The loch, the highest in all Scotland, was so firmly frozen and so deeply covered with drifted snow that it was difficult to realise that a sheet of deep water lay buried here. When first I looked the corrie and its loch were an unbroken expanse of white, but soon the dark form of a golden eagle sailed across from the west. The great bird was considerably below me and for a time sailed in spirals above the loch, but there was no encouragement to hunt here and so the eagle passed on eastward.

When I reached the corrie I found it lifeless as the hill plateau. No track of mountain hare, red-deer, or ptarmigan was visible on the snow here, for the depth of snow was such that the food supply was entirely cut off and all wild life had been driven to the lower grounds.

The ptarmigan seemed to have gone from the hills; it was not till I had reached the lower slopes that I saw the first pair of these hardy birds. The hen was still white; the cock had already grown the dark feathers of the summer dress, except on his breast. Near these birds a second pair of ptarmigan took wing, and now the tracks of fox and mountain hare were visible in the snow. The grouse were restless – a sure sign of a change of weather. They flew hither and thither in large packs as though the eagle were hunting, but I saw no signs of this bird.

The wind freshened, and near the summit of Brae Riach the powdery snow was caught up and whirled in thin clouds hundreds of feet above the hill-top. Over one cornice that fringed the precipice a small ethereal cloud of drift was being blown continuously out into space. Inconceivably fragile did this drifting snow appear; as it was carried into the frozen air it almost at once dissolved, as a cloud in the strengthening rays of the midsummer sun.

Thus I left the eagles' Arctic haunt as the April twilight came to the glen, and the frosty wind bound the peaty earth and formed a layer of ice upon the spray-drenched stones of the swiftly flowing hill burn, that added its music to the murmur of the pines at the edge of the forest.

CHAPTER 9

THE COUNTRY OF THE EAGLE

A Highland Forest in Spring

"The world is grown so bad,
That wrens make prey where eagles dare not perch." – SHAKESPEARE.

The forest is one of old storm-scarred pines, but amongst the pines are clusters of birches, and when she feels the breath of the warm south wind – the White Wind as the old Gaelic saying has it – the birch arrays herself in a delicate dress of filmy green. Seen against the sun-flood of an April noon each birch is a tree of burnished gold. In comparison the pines are sombre indeed, but they too send forth unobtrusively young flexible shoots of pale brown in which is their life's sap.

Well do these ancient pines know the fickleness of our northern spring. Have they not seen the snows drifting on the north wind even in May?

Spring-tide is scarcely the season of mushrooms, but there is one mushroom found in the Highland forests in spring, and that is the morel. It is crinkly and a very deep rich brown in colour, and as it thrusts its growing head through the dark soil amongst the trees it appears at first glance to be a small lump of peat. The morel mushroom is excellent eating, and in Germany is considered a great delicacy.

How clear is the air above the forest between the April showers! How delightful is the perfume from the young birch leaves in the sun-gleams that follow the rain! In olden times the maidens of the Highlands used to distill a perfume from the leaves of the birch. But one fears that they would not now be content with so natural a scent.

In the spring sunshine the forest lochs sparkle. Here handsome goosander drakes swim with their mates or fly swiftly from one feeding-ground to another. In the reed-beds wigeon court, and from the heathery shores of the lochs the greenshank's wild, tuneful music drifts down upon the breeze.

Beside the clear, alder-fringed pools the willow hangs out golden catkins; on sunny slopes the broom has already clothed herself with orange-coloured blossoms.

From the eagle's home far up the hillside one looks through the dark clustered pines on to the loch below. At first there is brilliant sunshine, then a shower of drifting hail forms swiftly, and a rainbow of brilliant colours is thrown across the loch. Beneath the fir trees beside the eagle's eyrie innumerable blaeberry plants are unfolding their green leaves, and amongst the leaves one sees here and there the small, rosy flower which in time will become the succulent dark-blue berry so eagerly sought after by the birds – and by the human race also.

One April when the eagle had her eyrie in the forest I reached the nest at noon and, concealed behind a tree, looked down upon the small fir beside a hill stream where the eagle was brooding her two handsome eggs. Hour after hour she sat there, and except that once she preened the feathers of one great wing she never stirred. A heavy shower of hail and snow passed across the forest from the high hills to the west, and when the sun again appeared it shone upon a world of white. Upon the eagle's back drops of water sparkled in the sun as she breathed slowly and rhythmically.

FORAGING.

And then, sailing swiftly up the corrie came her mate. With a rush of wings he alighted upon the branch of a tree beside her and stood there in the sunshine, a very king amongst birds. For perhaps a couple of minutes he remained, then gave himself a great shake (just as a dog might have done), spread his broad wings and sailed away.

Rising without a movement of his pinions, higher and ever higher into the blue vault of the sky he rode, a dark speck against the breeze, then closed his wings and stooped earthwards at terrific speed, alighting upon a fir tree beside the loch a thousand feet below. Immediately came a great outcry from some enraged and terrified jackdaws (I had seen the remains of a jackdaw in an eyrie the season before), and the eagle again rose into the air and mounted quickly. For long one of the jackdaws pursued him, making angry and puny darts at the eagle, who set his aerial course with supreme indifference to his small antagonist.

One was reminded of the old Celtic legend which tells that long, long ago, eagle and wren competed one against the other.

The eagle had boasted proudly that there was no single bird in all the world that could fly as high as he could. To his amazement the brown wren challenged him, and while all the bird world looked on the two commenced their trial of strength. The eagle mounted, as is his custom, in great circles and spirals, but the wren flew straight towards the zenith, and since be had the advantage at first, he was able to alight unperceived upon the eagle's back when he was tired. At last the eagle, at an immense height, was weary (he would scarcely have risen so high had not all the rest of the birds been watching him). He called out, expecting no answer, "C'aite bheil thu, dhreolan?" "Where are you now, little wren?" To his amazement from his back came a shrill small voice, " Tha mise an so do cheann." "I am here above your head." And so it was the wren and not the eagle that was the victor and was made King of Birds.

CHAPTER 10

A WEST HIGHLAND EYRIE

"There be three things which are too wonderful for me, yea, four which I know not: The way of an eagle in the air; the way of a serpent upon a rock; the way of a ship in the midst of the sea; and the way of a man with a maid." – Proverbs XXX.18, 19.

One spring day a few years ago the mist was unusually close on the hill. The sea-loch lay placid as a mirror, except where the strong flood tide was forcing its way westward. From a stone at the margin of the tide a greenshank rose and flew across the loch, throwing its wild call-notes to the silent hills.

Up a steep birch-clad hill I climbed, across a ridge by way of a *bealach* or hill pass, and then to the top of a gorge through which a hill burn dropped in grey waterfalls to the glen below. There were rowans and birches in this gorge, and a golden eagle had built her eyrie at the foot of one of these birches, where it grew out in a curve from the steep slope above the gorge. The eagle was brooding on her nest when I stood on the cliff above; when she saw me, after a momentary fierce glance she launched herself into space and sailed away across the hill. In the eyrie was an eaglet about a week old and an addled egg. Two lambs and a rabbit were lying in the nest. The date was 10th May, and the eaglet had probably hatched on the 3rd of that month, which is the average date of hatching on the lower grounds.

About seventeen feet from the eyrie was a small grassy ledge and it was here that the hide was ultimately placed. The first day a few green birch branches were cut and laid in position on the ledge, in order that the eagles might gradually become used to something strange near the nest.

For seven days the eyrie was left undisturbed, and then one morning, when the dun wind of the west was sweeping the grey clouds low over the hill, three of us – the shepherd, my wife, and myself – crossed the pass and descended the western bank of the eagle's gorge. The eagle for a moment looked up at us with annoyance, then launched herself out into space. She was, for a golden eagle, an unusually tame bird, and soon settled upon a rock about three hundred yards away. There she stood watching us setting up our hiding-tent and covering it with green birch branches. The ledge on which the hide was built was a narrow one, and there was only just room enough for a person to crouch in the hiding-tent with the photographic apparatus. At a few minutes past ten o'clock my wife began the first watch in the hide, and, in order to distract the attention of the eagle, the shepherd with his two dogs walked towards the rock on which she was perched, while I, with our collie Dileas, walked down to the glen below. The shepherd crossed the ridge and disappeared from sight; I climbed some miles up the glen and waited there most of the day.

At four o'clock in the afternoon I walked down the glen to a place where I could "spy" the nest, and to my delight I saw that the eagle was brooding quietly on her eyrie. She was evidently unsuspicious of the hiding-tent, because she was looking away from it and down towards the glen below. I thereupon climbed the hill and, keeping out of sight of the eyrie, approached it from above at a quarter to five o'clock. On seeing me the eagle flew out heavily from the nest and alighted upon the rock she had perched on that morning. My wife had been in the cramped quarters of the hide for six and a half hours. She was so stiff and cold that at first she was unable to stand erect, and had to massage her knees before she could climb up the almost perpendicular face of the gorge. The following notes, written in the hiding-tent by the observer during her long and cold watch, give a vivid account of what occurred:

"10.40 a.m. B.S.T. Mist and rain. The eaglet is cheeping and lying still in the eyrie. I hear the following birds in song: missel-thrush, wren, willow-warbler, chaffinch, redstart, and ring-ousel. The eaglet cheeps continuously,' Swee, swee, swee; tlui, tlui, tlui' 11.30 a.m. The mother eagle arrives at her eyrie. She alights on a branch of the tree and then hops down into the nest. She picks up something from beneath the eaglet and eats it. Then slowly, with extreme care, she lowers herself over the eaglet to brood it. The eaglet's cheeping ceases immediately. She sits with her back to me, her head-feathers fluffed up. She seems to have no suspicions of the hiding-tent or any idea that I am concealed within it. 11.45 a.m. A stone, perhaps dislodged by a grazing sheep, falls down the gorge. The eagle looks round angrily. 12 noon. She seems to be expecting or hearing something – perhaps her mate and looks all around her very eagerly. There are the remains of four lambs in the eyrie, but the shepherd believes them all to have been dead when taken by the eagle, because the lambing-time this season has been a bad one, and there has been great mortality among lambs. At 12.55 p.m. the eagle stands up and walks across to one of the lambs. She tears off small morsels of flesh and, very, very gently for so large and fierce a bird, reaches over to her chick and hands it the morsels one by one. If the piece of meat is too large for the small eagle to swallow she eats it herself. For fifteen minutes she feeds the eaglet, then settles down to brood it again. 1.15 p.m. It is raining heavily. The eagle is very still. There is a robin singing quite near. The mother eagle yawns occasionally, and from time to time looks down and under her, perhaps to see if her chick is awake (as she is brooding with her back towards me I cannot see exactly what she is doing). 2.35p.m. The mother eagle closes her eyes and sleeps. Her head droops in slumber. The rain continues. Suddenly a redstart bursts into song a few feet away. The eagle wakes with a start, fiercely annoyed that she should be disturbed thus. 2.43 p.m. The eagle listens and looks up."

(About this time I had seen the cock eagle pass across the glen, and the sitting bird was evidently looking up at him.)

At five o'clock we left the eyrie and crossed the pass. In the glen where we were staying with the shepherd and his wife tree pipits were mounting in song above the sweet-smelling birches, and soon a gentle rain commenced to fall and the mist dropped low on the hills.

There was brilliant sunshine next morning, and as we climbed the steep hillside the heat was intense. When we reached the head of the gorge the eagle was sailing below us across the hill, and when she saw us she flew over to her accustomed perch.

Today I took the watch in the hiding-tent, and at 10.40 a.m. was shut in by my wife, who walked on with our collie to distract the eagle's attention. The eaglet was obviously growing. He was much happier today and dozed in the warm sun, and sometimes played with the lining of the nest. I had been in the hide just half an hour when the mother eagle suddenly appeared. She stood at the edge of the eyrie not more than fifteen feet from me, a glorious bird with the May sunshine full upon her. She at once commenced to tear small pieces off one of the lambs and feed both herself and her eaglet. She remained at the nest for three-quarters of an hour, then with a sweep of her great wings vanished from my sight. In twenty-five minutes she was back, and was obviously entirely unaware of my presence in the hide. She rummaged on the floor of the eyrie, picking up and eating small white objects. Perhaps they were ticks, or maggots from the sheep. This done, she brooded the eaglet. It was charming to see the care she lavished upon her only child. Very gently she walked towards it, her legs wide apart and bent outwards, her claws folded in lest she might inadvertently injure the fragile life in her charge. At 2.05 p.m. she seemed to be listening to something and, walking to the edge of the eyrie, launched out into the air. In twenty-five minutes she was back. Again she fed the youngster on the lamb, and it was interesting to see that the eaglet seemed unable to judge distances, for it often made ineffective pecks at the food its mother held towards it. The mother showed infinite patience with the eaglet, and it was surprising to see how much food she coaxed it to swallow.

At 2.50 p.m. the eagle once more left the eyrie carrying with her the remains of the lamb's leg. In two minutes she returned and brooded her young. Again she rooted about in the lining of the eyrie before settling down, and picked up a fouled stick but did not remove it. As she mothered the eaglet she bent down to it from time to time and fondled its small downy head. The sun was now shining into the nest with intense heat, and the brooding eagle pecked at the small flies that danced above her head; the sun made her pant and gasp for breath. The eaglet slept. It lay half beneath its mother, its small head pillowed on a branch. Suddenly a sheep "meeh-ed" near. The eagle glared fiercely in the direction of that sound, for she no doubt associated the cry of the sheep with the approach of the shepherd. She left the nest at seven minutes to four o'clock.

At 4.50 p.m. the eagle returned to her eyrie, bringing with her a large bunch of heather. She commenced to feed hungrily on the lamb, from time to time handing dainty pieces to the eaglet. Then, with much effort, she gulped down a bone of considerable size; it seemed as if it must certainly stick in her throat! She brooded her young awhile, then searched long and carefully in the lining of the nest, picking up and swallowing small objects. As she did this she swallowed by mistake a piece of stick, which gave her considerable discomfort for some time.

At 5.18 p.m. the eagle made an upward spring from the eyrie and sailed out over the glen; she had not returned when, at 6.10 p.m., my wife arrived to liberate me from my cramped quarters.

Her narrative supplemented my own observations. At four o'clock she had seen an eagle, probably the bird which had left the eyrie at 3.53 pm., perched upon the topmost point of a hill 3000 feet high and just across the glen. As she watched, the eagle soared out from her lofty perch and, without a movement of the wings, rose a full 3000 feet above the hill-top. Suddenly she was seen to close her wings and drop earthward at stupendous speed. In three headlong dives she fell, checking herself momentarily between the stoops. She reached the eyrie just six seconds after she had first closed her wings. Now the nest was approximately 1100 feet above sea-level, and so she had dropped some 5000 feet in the incredibly short time of six seconds!

At half past five my wife noticed that my eagle, which had left the nest at 5.18 p.m., was perched on her favourite knoll, preening

Hen eagle brooding in a rain shower. Note raindrops on her plumage.

her feathers. She suddenly rose and flew west. At a great height she met two eagles flying in from the west. One of the eagles joined her, the other turned, and flew in the direction whence it had come. Now it was a curious thing that, during the three days we kept watch at the eyrie, the cock bird never once came to the nest. Could it have been that he had partly deserted his wife and was spending most of his time with another lady?

As we crossed the ridge above the nest that evening we saw the eagle appear above the eyrie. She was being mobbed by a peregrine falcon, but seemed to ignore the smaller bird. There were no grouse near that eyrie, and no hares. Even the rabbit was absent. Thus, since she had no mate to help her in her hunting, it must have been difficult for the eagle to find food for the eaglet. During the whole time we watched the eyrie no prey of any kind was brought in. The lambs each day became "higher," until their smell was quite unpleasant when the breeze blew from the eyrie to the watcher in the hide. And yet the tiny eaglet was fed on this very high meat, and seemed to thrive upon it.

Five days later the shepherd visited the eyrie. He found a freshly plucked ptarmigan in the nest, but of the eaglet there was no sign, and some mischance had befallen it. Whatever disaster had overtaken it must have occurred that day, because the ptarmigan had not been many hours in the eyrie when the shepherd handled it.

We shall long remember the last evening of the watch in the hide. The breeze had dropped. The sky was full of soft clouds. Each hill, glen, and corrie was bathed in the glow of the westering sun. Fifteen hundred feet beneath us lay a sea-loch. Here there was wind, for we could see the waves breaking on the shore of pebbles beside wild cherry trees heavy with snowy blossoms. From time to time the aroma from the birches in the glen was wafted up to us, and the scent of the *roid* or bog myrtle. The sun set, and then the full moon shone out over the glen, and the scent of many plants was in the air – the perfume of primroses, the fragrance of the larch, the bog myrtle, and the birch.

CHAPTER 11

THE COUNTRY OF THE EAGLE

THE FIONN LEIRG AND ITS TWELVE SHIELINGS

"But they that wait upon the Lord shall renew their strength, they shall mount up with
wings as eagles " – Isaiah xl. 31.

From dark Loch Tulla in the Blackmount Forest across to
Glen Strae and thence to the shore of Loch Awe the Fionn
Leirg (the Fair Pass) leads. It is a lonely track, and no
occupied dwelling is in sight throughout its length, but upon the
watershed, at the very head of the pass, are clustered the ruins of
twelve small shielings.

One April morning when I left Loch Tulla the sun was shining
brightly and the air was tense and vital. The ground was crisp
with frost; weeks of drought had shrunk the river Orchy until it
was far below summer level. Around Loch Tulla splendid old pine

trees stand. From them, the western outposts of the old Caledonian Forest, a delicious scent was being drawn by the sun's rays. An old blackcock rose ahead of me and flew up to the dense crowning foliage of one of the firs to conceal himself.

The loch lay like a sheet of glass; it seemed to sleep in the strong sunlight. At first glance it appeared deserted, but looking more closely I saw many birds upon its quiet waters. Wigeon, golden-eye, goosander, and mallard were all feeding there, and once the silence was broken by the deep-toned fluting of a green-shank as a pair of these birds crossed the loch in swift flight. Curlews and oyster-catchers flew overhead, full of the joy of life; on the loch a golden-eye drake was courting his mate, and as he circled round her the sun shone upon his creamy breast and flanks so that he appeared almost as white as a sea-gull.

As I entered Glen Euar the snowy cone of Ben Cruachan glistened far to the west; nearer at hand the conical peak of Stob Choire an Albannaich rose white from the lonely shore of Loch Dochart. In Glen Euar are veteran pines scarred and twisted by many a winter's storm, but soon I had entered a treeless world with brown grass and peat hags and, here and there, a lingering snow-wreath. How silent are the hills, glens, and passes of the Blackmount Forest! Grouse are scarce, and the curlew, who throws his wild music far across the lower glens at this season of spring, does not visit the higher ground. No sad-toned fluting of golden plover breaks the stillness thus high.

I had little thoughts of human dwellings in this country of silence, but suddenly, in as lonely a spot as could well be imagined, I saw, on a little clearing beside a burn, the ruins of twelve shielings. They were clustered together, the remnants of small, humble dwellings, yet they stood for a part of the lives of the people of the Highlands, which is now scarcely a memory. No one living can tell their history. Their age must be well over a hundred years. It is thought they were the summer shielings of the crofters who lived in Glen Strae, or perhaps upon the shores of Loch Awe.

Long years ago a busy community must have journeyed each year to this lonely spot 1500 feet above the level of the Atlantic. Around the shielings cattle and sheep would doubtless have been pastured on the green hill grass, and of an evening Gaelic airs would have been sung, and perhaps a tune on the clarsach or piob mhor played. The summer days at the shielings must have passed quickly. There was butter to be churned, cheese to be made, wool to be picked and carded. The young folk perhaps roamed the hills and fished for trout in the small clear burns, or scaled the cliffs of Beinn Suidhe for the ravens' young.

Now the eagle soars above the deserted shielings and the ravens of Beinn Suidhe nest in peace. This April day I saw one of the ravens furiously pursue a bird of his kind that had ventured on his nesting territory and, having seen the intruder off his beat, fly swiftly towards his nest on the cliffs of Beinn Suidhe. A peregrine falcon passed overhead. With mad, exulting flight it stooped earthward, then hovered awhile like some great kestrel.

From the land of the summer shielings I could see Loch Awe sparkling in the sunlight, a thin haze from the smoke of many fires lying above its waters. East were Loch Tulla and its encircling pines, beyond which Beinn Dorain rose steeply. North, south, east, and west creamy smoke from many heather fires rose lazily to an immense height, then spread cloud-like over the sky.

It was now afternoon, and with the thawing of the springs each small burn was rising. Upon the great expanse of brown hill grass in the Fionn Leirg the sun shone with almost painful intensity. The snowy tops of the big hills shimmered in the heat haze. The view was a very fair one, for the west was in her magic mood. Yet it was a silent country of past memories that I crossed that evening, and heard beside Loch Tulla the trilling of curlew, the pipe of oyster-catchers, and the whistling of wigeon.

CHAPTER 12

THE COUNTRY OF THE EAGLE

A LOCHABER DEER FOREST IN MAY

"Faint sound of eagle melting into blue." – Wordsworth.

Across the glens of the west the spirit of spring early throws her creative mantle. It was delightful, therefore, to leave the uplands of Inverness-shire brown almost as in midwinter, and late that day reach the softer climate of Lochaber. Here, beside the sparkling waters of Loch Linnhe, the birches had arrayed themselves in their delicate tracery and the primrose scented the May air. In the woods many birds made music. The loud-ringing notes of the missel-thrush mingled with the songs of chaffinch and mavis, and willow-warblers, newly arrived from overseas, uttered a soft and very musical spray of song. From the shore came the pipe of oyster-catchers and the deeper flute-like call of a greenshank. On sunny banks the broom was already showing its golden blossom; the young fronds of the bracken were uncurling, and amongst them were pools of blue where the wild violet blossomed. Upon the quiet waters of Loch Linnhe a great northern diver, on passage northward to his nesting tarn in distant Iceland, could be seen at his fishing, and orange-billed herons stood at the margin of the flood-tide, awaiting patiently any fish that might unwarily swim within range of their lance-like bills.

In the Central Highlands the deer forests stand high; in the west they often descend to sea-level. There are ravens in most of these western forests, and one sunny morning I crossed with my host to a cliff that dropped sheer from the heather-covered hillside to the sea beneath. Far below us was a nestful of young ravens, almost ready to fly. In the stiff northerly breeze the parent ravens soared above us, uttering from time to time short, anxious croaks. Beneath us, tossing upon the white-crested waves of the sea-loch, salmon fishermen were examining their nets. Each season a pair of ravens nest on this sea-cliff. Some years ago the keeper shot the hen raven as she left the nest. A short time later the cock visited the nest and, seeing the eggs were unharmed, flew away across the sea-loch. In a few hours he returned, escorting a new wife to his home, and she trustingly took up the duties of hatching the eggs at once!

Above the cliff of the ravens a small loch lies. Here sand-pipers called and a pair of handsome red-throated divers swam together. In the birch woods hinds were feeding, and a roe-buck and his doe were near them.

Westward we walked up a grassy glen. Here there was shelter from the north wind and the sun shone warmly, so that it was delightful to lie in comfort and "spy" with the long glass across to a great rock where a pair of eagles had their eyrie. The hen today was hunting above the hill-face opposite the nest; her mate brooded the downy young in the eyrie. At length he rose, stood over the two youngsters awhile, then, after looking fiercely out over the glen, launched himself into the air. Leaning on the wind, with wings motionless, he quickly reached a height of fully two thousand feet. As we watched him there it seemed as if, far above him, a small white bird soared, and we remembered the old Gaelic legend that somewhere there lived a single white-plumaged bird who was king of all the feathered tribes. Then gradually we realised that this was no bird, but a planet of unusual brilliance that shone clearly even in the strong sunlight of a May noon.

Soon the eagle half closed his great wings and sped westward towards his hunting-grounds.

Near the head of the glen a *bealach* or pass crosses the hills. The ascent was steep, the sun was hot, but up this *bealach* my host, fleet of foot on the hills of his ancestors, set a desperate pace, so that it was pleasant to halt near the crest of the pass. Here the heather was stunted, and amongst it grew the fox's weed, as the club-moss is known in the west. In olden times the club-moss was believed by the people of the Isles to act as a charm. There is a rhyme —

> "Garbhag an t-sleibh air mo shiubhal,
> Cha'n eirich domh beud no pudhar,
> Cha mharbh garmaisg cha dearg iubhar mi,
> Cha riab grianuisg no glaislig uidhir mi."

> "The club-moss is on my person,
> No harm nor mishap can me befall,
> No sprite shall slay me, no arrow shall wound me,
> No fay nor dun water-nymph shall tear me." [*]

From the crest of the *bealach* we looked across the glen to the eagles' eyrie, now a considerable distance away. Through the glass one of the eagles could be seen feeding the young; the eaglets at that distance seemed like two small white specks. Far beneath us was the sea. Like drifting snowflakes sea-gulls circled above their nesting islands. Westward two herring drifters passed, steering from the Caledonian Canal to western fishing-grounds in the Atlantic. Far to the south the twin peaks of Cruachan rose. The sun shone on these snowy cones and upon the white summit of Ben Nevis, but driving snow squalls hid the hills of the Blackmount Forest and the peaks of Glencoe. Beneath us, to the east, was a broad glen. We descended to this glen, passing a few of the old Scots pines that in past centuries extended in an almost unbroken forest from the shores of the Atlantic to Rothiemurchus, Mar, Balmoral, Glen Tana, and

[*] *Carmina gadelica*

Finzean. But the trees of the western country do not now cover the glens thickly as in the Central Highlands. They are found as stragglers, mainly in hollows beside small hill streams where they are sheltered from the Atlantic gales. The trees are all very old, and unless the hillsides on which they are growing are fenced in the pines will soon be extinct, for sheep and red deer devour the seedlings, and the old trees cannot live forever.

We reached the glen and passed down it through birch woods above which curlews made sad music. Many deer were grazing on the young grass here; the scent of birch leaves was in the air. At Tobair na Banaraich we drank of the clear waters of this, the Milkmaid's Well, then set out homeward through a keen air that at sunset brought frost to the country of the west.

CHAPTER 13

THE COUNTRY OF THE EAGLE

Ben Cruachan in snow

There is an old tradition in Argyll that the ever-youthful witch, by name Cailleach Bheur, each morning walked from the Mull of Cantyre to the summit of Ben Cruachan. She made light of that great walk, and before the sun had topped the heights eastward had driven her cow to a certain well near the hill top. The cow, having drunk of the magic waters of this well, was rejuvenated, and after grazing awhile upon the scanty alpine vegetation was driven home in the gloaming to her byre on the Mull of Cantyre.

One May morning, when the air was keen as of a March day, I left the swiftly flowing Awe, where the oaks were bronze with young foliage, and set my face for the country of the eagle on the upper slopes of Ben Cruachan. Amongst the grass many violets showed

86

and here and there the rose-coloured flowers of the lousewort, while from the russet tangle of old bracken the young green fern fronds were pressing upwards. Upon the boulders wheatears "chacked," and meadow pipits mounted into the sunny air to sail earthward in song.

At 2000 feet the snowline was reached. At first the ground was covered thinly, but soon I was wading through deep snowfields, on which the sun shone so brilliantly that the eye could scarcely look upon them.

Far below me the Awe, a silvery line in the sunshine, flowed swiftly towards Loch Etive. On the turbulent Earrach pool a lady could be seen plying her rod; upon the more placid waters of Linne na Churraich another angler toiled.

On the ridge at the head of a grassy corrie I halted awhile. Thus high no grouse crowed, no wheatear called; even the last of the hill sheep had been left behind. The small burns here flowed partly beneath the snow, and a lochan was buried below the snow that lay upon the ice. The tracks of a fox, made perhaps a couple of days previously, crossed the snowy expanse.

Above me towered Stob Dearg, the west top of Cruachan, its cone thickly plastered with snow. Northward Loch Etive crept eastward into the hills. The sands at its head gleamed in the sun; its waters reflected the deep blue of the sky.

Loch Etive for the Gael must always be a country of romance, for here Deirdre, the ideal of Celtic womanhood, lived happily with Naois, one of the Sons of Uisne. In the old royal forest of Dal an Eas or Dalness of Glen Etive, Naois, with Deirdre by his side, swift footed as Diana of old, hunted the red deer. By the shore of the loch was her *grianan* or bower; her home was protected by the magic luis, or quicken trees. The late Dr Alexander Carmichael, the foremost authority on Gaelic lore of his time, tells us the old people who lived on the sides and at the head of Loch Etive spoke much of Deirdre. She was known to them as "Deirdre of the fair skin," whose locks were more auburn than the western gold of the summer sun. The old people had a tradition that the *grianan* of Deirdre was thatched with the royal fern and lined with the pine of the hills and the downy feathers of birds. But now the old people are gone from Loch Etive, and there is scarcely a family living along its upper shores.

A WEST HIGLAND EYRIE. THE HEN EAGLE IS LOOKING TOWARDS THE HIDING-TENT. HER
FEET ARE HIDDEN BY THE LAMBS' CARCASES ON WHICH SHE IS STANDING.

Today a golden eagle rose from the topmost cairn of Ben Cruachan as I approached it. He mounted high, then steered northward, towards the land where, long ago, Naois and Deirdre lived.

It was early afternoon when I reached the summit of Ben Cruachan. Here the snow lay thick, and the north-facing side of each boulder was encrusted with feathery ice-crystals. No breath of wind stirred. To the south the air was hazy; north and east the weather was fine and the sky deep blue, with light fleecy clouds drifting gently across it.

On the far eastern horizon rose a group of flat-topped mountains, which caught my eye by reason of the immense amount of snow they carried. This distant snowy expanse gleamed golden in the May sunlight; it had all the appearance of the ice-capped hills of north Spitsbergen as seen from the Greenland Ocean. The unaided eye saw merely a vague range of hills; a telescope revealed them as the Cairngorms.

It was interesting to see these mountains of the Central Highlands from a hill of the western seaboard a full seventy miles distant. Brae Riach showed no single speck of black upon all its wide slopes; the burn in Clais Luineag flowed entirely beneath the snow. I thought of the ptarmigan and their eggs, and wondered what effect that unprecedented May snowstorm would have upon them. Later on, when in the Cairngorms in early July, I found the ptarmigan still sitting on eggs, which must have been second layings.

Upon Ben Nevis the snowy covering did not extend so low, but the hill-top was of unbroken white.

North-west, above the haze that was gathering there, the hills of Rhum rose dimly; through a gap in the nearer hills I could see the snowy slopes of the Cuillin of Skye.

South and south-west distant Arran, Jura, and Colonsay showed faintly.

On the Atlantic many craft could be seen. Between Colonsay and Lochbuie, in the Isle of Mull, the smoke of a steamer rose. Through the Sound of Mull herring drifters were hurrying for the market at Oban.

How far a cry is it from Arran, Colonsay, Rhum, and Skye of the west to the snowy slopes of the Cairngorm hills in Aberdeenshire;

from Ben Lomond, in sight of Glasgow, to the Ross-shire peaks! Yet by merely turning the head all that immense stretch of country could be seen.

That evening there was pleasant warmth beside the swiftly flowing Awe, and in the air above the river was the scent of countless primroses; but at the eagle's haunt on Ben Cruachan frost and snow lingered until June had come.

CHAPTER 14

EAGLES, GROUSE PRESERVING AND SHEEP FARMING

The golden eagle will never be permitted to increase where there are grouse moors. A well-known Highland laird said to me not long ago, "Pay me so much for each pair of golden eagles and each pair of peregrine falcons, and I shall be delighted to keep them on my ground." That, I think, is a reasonable view, and with regard to the peregrine there is nothing that can be said in its favour except that it is a magnificent bird – dashing, fearless, swift, and impetuous. The eagle takes grouse, but they are not his staple food, and where blue hares are plentiful on a moor the eagle always captures them in preference to grouse.

I know one or two grouse moors – they are large moors, and one is partly a deer forest – where the golden eagle is left undisturbed, and I do not think the bags on these moors are greatly affected by the presence of the eagles.

From my own observations, and from the information given

91

me by many friends and correspondents, there is no doubt that the harm an eagle does on a grouse moor during the shooting season consists, not so much in the grouse he eats, as in his habit of sailing over a hillside and moving every single grouse off it. Grouse drives are frequently spoiled by the appearance of an eagle, and so keepers have little reason to love him. Is it not remarkable that grouse should have such a dread of the eagle? They will entirely ignore beaters and guns when the king of birds appears on the scene.

A peregrine falcon strikes his prey in the air, so when he is near, grouse lie like stones. A golden eagle almost always captures his prey on the ground, and so grouse, when they see him, instinctively take wing, and fly in confusion at a great height – far higher than when they are driven. Thus, although he may not catch, or even pursue, a single grouse, an eagle may do more harm to a grouse drive than a peregrine, who will kill a grouse in full view of the guns.

There are, however, some good sportsmen to whom a heavy bag of grouse is not everything in this life, and who are generous enough to allow the eagle to remain because he adds a great charm to the hills and corries, and takes a diseased or sickly grouse in preference to one in perfect health.

I have nothing but admiration for those proprietors of what may be termed mixed grouse-moor and deer-forest land who issue strict orders to their keepers to preserve not only the eagles themselves but also their eggs and young.

Besides taking grouse, however, the golden eagle preys upon birds and animals that are destructive to grouse and are termed "vermin". I myself have seen at an eagle's eyrie a stoat, a jackdaw, and several squirrels, while rats, fox cubs, ravens, and grey crows have from time to time been found at an eagle's nest. One season a pair of eagles nested, and reared two eaglets, on a grouse moor without the owner being aware of the fact, and I do not think that his bag of grouse suffered at all that autumn. Of this I am quite sure, that the grey or hooded crow is a far more deadly enemy to red grouse than the golden eagle. One has only to walk near where a pair of hooded crows have their nest to see the toll they take of eggs. Sucked eggs lie everywhere, for each day the crows search the moors with extreme thoroughness for nesting grouse, and are marvelously clever in locating the nests. They take grouse chicks also, and so, bird for bird, they do at least as much harm as the eagle. It must be remembered, too, that on the average large Scottish grouse moor there are at least a dozen pairs of hooded crows for every pair of golden eagles.

The amount of harm eagles do on a sheep-farm is very difficult to compute, and although some shepherds and sheep-farmers regard the eagle as the enemy of young lambs, I am convinced that it is only exceptionally that eagles take *living* lambs. The golden eagle is fond of carrion of all sorts, and a dead lamb on a dark hillside cannot fail to attract him. A certain number of lambs are born dead every spring, and when a snowstorm or much cold, wet weather is experienced during the lambing season the mortality is great. To see a lamb in an eagle's eyrie is sufficient proof to many shepherds that eagles are taking their living lambs. They do not stop to think whether the lamb was dead before it was carried to the eyrie. I shall always remember the fairness of one shepherd who showed me an eagle's eyrie in which no fewer than four lambs were lying. Far from showing signs of annoyance, the shepherd told me he was convinced that all these lambs had been dead when they had been taken by the eagle, for, he said, the mortality among lambs had been unusually great that spring. But would not the average shepherd, after seeing four lambs at an eyrie, have been the eagle's sworn enemy for life? On less evidence than this a friend of mine put a black mark against the pair of eagles that were nesting on his ground. A number of his lambs went amissing. A fox might have taken them, or they might have succumbed to any of the many dangers that beset the very young. My friend, however, was convinced that they had been killed by the eagles. Perhaps they had been so taken; more likely they had not. There was no proof either way. I have asked many shepherds and keepers whether they have ever seen a golden eagle take a live lamb, and few have ever seen this. A friend of mine, a great naturalist and sheep-farmer with wide experience, believes that certain eagles may form the habit of taking lambs, just as certain lions form the habit of killing men. Such a lion is known as a man-eating lion, and my friend believes – and I agree with him – that certain eagles become lamb-eating eagles. He writes: "I do not think that the golden eagles on my sheep-farm in the Isle of Mull ever touched a lamb, either alive or dead. Dead lambs were frequently lying within a few hundred yards of the nest but were never touched by the eagles, and not a particle of wool was to be found in the eyrie. The mountain hare was plentiful on all the hills around, and hares were the eagles' chief food.

"My father, grandfather, and mother's brother had large sheep-farms in the Rannoch, Loch Eil, and Loch Arkaig districts respectively, where eagles were fairly common, but I have never heard them complain of loss of lambs from eagles. I have not the slightest doubt that some eagles may learn the habit of taking lambs, yet I think it is very uncommon, and if hares are numerous eagles very seldom do harm to either game or lambs."

To sum up, both from my own experience and from the many letters which I have received from correspondents, I think it is only when food is scarce that eagles take lambs, and that out of every hundred lambs taken by eagles ninety-nine are dead when taken.

The fondness of the eagle for the body of any dead animal is well known. A stag that has died out on the hillside is shared by fox and eagle; there is no more deadly bait for an eagle than a dead cat. The only wonder is that eagles take lambs so seldom as they do.

Grouse the eagle takes as his right, but in the old days, when eagles and other birds of prey were numerous throughout the Highlands of Scotland, there were many more grouse along the western seaboard and in the Hebridean Isles than there are now.

There was no grouse disease in those days because the balance of nature had not been disturbed, and any weakly grouse was soon accounted for. Nowadays grouse in most places lead an artificial life, for all their enemies are ruthlessly exterminated. On the first-class grouse moors there are undoubtedly far more grouse than in earlier days, and huge bags are made. But that mysterious and deadly ailment, grouse disease, is liable suddenly to decimate a moor, and the heavier the stock of birds the greater the ravages of the disease.

One has only to read the late Osgood MacKenzie of Inverewe's book, *A Hundred Years in the Highlands*, to realise the difference between grouse shooting fifty years ago and at the present day. Then the sportsman was content with a small bag and worked hard for it. He went out with his dogs, spent the night at some lonely bothy far up among the hills, and was on foot at dawn. Nowadays the tendency is towards making grouse shooting too easy. There are roads even to the most outlying beat, along which the sportsman travels at great speed in his comfortable car. There are ponies to meet him, there is a hot lunch spread out upon a snowy tablecloth for him to enjoy, and he is not satisfied unless the bag be a very heavy one. I do not suggest that all sportsmen shoot thus. I have a friend who realises that nothing obtained easily, without effort, can give real or lasting satisfaction, and although he could shoot his grouse without exertion he spends long days afoot on the hill, tramping many miles up the glens and across the tops.

Those who shirk discomfort and hardship have no idea what they miss: the curling mist rising from the glen at sunrise, the flight of the white-winged ptarmigan, the grey delicacy of the first autumn snows on the high tops. Their bags of grouse may be big, but in making them they miss some of the big things of life that the solitude of the high places makes all the bigger.

I will here quote a few from the many letters I have received from stalkers and others on the question of the eagle and game preserving.

A stalker of experience writes: "There is no doubt of the heavy toll of grouse an eagle takes. In good grouse seasons the balance of nature holds, but in a succession of bad seasons with reduced stocks the requirements of the eagle tell heavily. I often read of a dread of extinction, but I can assure you that on this range, and right west to the coast, there are more eagles than people have any idea of. Another point I would like to impress is that in my forty years' experience on the Grampian Range I have never known of a keeper violating the general estate rule in interfering with eagle eggs. Personally I like the eagle, the finest specimen of British birds, and find him a most useful and diverting topic of discussion on appearing out of the mist on an unpropitious stalking day. Again I have known an imaginary eagle account for a bad drive!" Another observant stalker writes: " I do not think eagles prey very heavily on grouse except when feeding their young. I have seen as many as seven grouse at an eyrie. Contrary to what many writers say about the King of Birds, I consider the eagle the most cowardly of birds. It has not a fraction of the dash and courage of that plucky little pirate of the air, the peregrine. Eagles have increased considerably of late years. The average game preserver has no reason to love the eagle, but, to their credit be it said, eagles are let out of traps when caught."

Another stalker writes: "Four pairs have nested in this district yearly for forty years. Most of them rear one young one yearly, and the eggs are rarely taken by egg collectors, but there is no general increase."

The head keeper on a western grouse moor writes: "It is not what the eagles kill that I object to; it is the way they scare the grouse so that they desert the ground an eagle frequents. There is proof of that here. The grouse beat of K— used to be good for 150 to 180 brace, and now 20 to 25 is its bag. Certainly there have been bad hatching seasons in the years 1919 to 1924, but 1925 and 1926 were good. On 26th August when the moor was shot an eagle was soaring over it and the grouse would scarcely rise, only flutter along the top of the heather." This seems to be contrary to the usual experience, which is the eagle sends the grouse away at a great height for a long distance, and sometimes to a neighbouring moor. Another correspondent writes: "When I was a boy there were still lots of grouse in G— due to a rigorous suppression of the hawk tribe. In 1855, 900 brace were got. Now not one is shot."

Over the whole of the west – the mainland of Scotland, the Inner Hebrides, and even the Outer Hebrides – there has been a great decrease of grouse during recent years. Many keepers and landowners believe that this decrease is due to the increase of so-called "vermin" but eagle, raven, and hooded crow were *always* present on these western grouse moors, and I am inclined to think that a change of climate, and not an increase in their enemies, is the reason for the decrease of grouse in the west.

One of the most interesting letters I have received is from Robert Burns, a keeper in Ross-shire. He writes: "For the last thirty years I have had many opportunities of watching eagles at work, and during all that period I have never seen an eagle take, or attempt to take, a grouse in the air or otherwise. That eagles do take grouse I am certain, though I think only for a short period of the year. In the years since the War I have paid particular attention to the finding of as many grouse nests as I can find time for, and on an

EAGLET ON ITS CLIFF-SIDE EYRIE.

average each May I have marked, along with the other men, roughly forty nests. Beginning with 1920, we found that a few of the grouse hens were taken off their nests by an eagle, plucked beside the nest, cleaned out, and carried away. Even a gamekeeper would not have put that down to the work of an eagle, but we found that sometimes an eagle's feather was beside the nest, and that sometimes droppings were beside the feathers. That taking of grouse hens went on until 1924. Neither in 1925 nor in 1926 did we know of a single sitting grouse taken by the eagle, although an eagle, or eagles, were on the ground every day. I have never seen any of the grouse's eggs broken or disturbed; the birds on every occasion were killed and plucked within a foot and less of the nest.

"The reason why these grouse were taken in the years 1920 to 1924 was, I am certain, the great scarcity of rabbits and mountain hares, which had become more or less extinct in the year 1916, and did not begin to increase until 1925. To see an eagle pick a hare off a hill-face without touching the ground is very neatly done for so clumsy-looking a bird." Burns continues: "I have listened to many conversations with keepers about eagles and grouse, and I have never met a keeper who grudged the eagle the grouse it takes, although eagles on a grouse moor, especially on driving days, are so aggravating that it is little wonder some of the keepers are up against them. Still I think that if there was any danger of the golden eagle becoming very scarce, the keeper would be one of the first to step in to protect the king of British birds.

"If ever the eagle should come on evil days, which I don't think there is any fear of, sure enough the professional egg collector and not the gamekeeper will be the greatest enemy."

I have only one record of an eagle attacking a sheep. It is from Donald Ross, and he writes: "About ten years ago I was out looking for foxes in Sutherlandshire, and on coming in on the top of a very rough, rocky corrie I saw an eagle rise about one hundred yards away.

"I noticed a bunch of wool fall from its talons, and on reaching the spot where the eagle had risen I found a Cheviot gimmer wedged in between two rocks. She was still alive, and the wool was partly torn from her back. There were a few gashes in the top of her shoulders – done by the eagle's beak. If I had not come on the

A WEST HIGHLAND EYRIE. THE SOLITARY EAGLET IS ABOUT A WEEK OLD.

scene I am quite sure the eagle would have had a good meal of her there and then.

"There is hardly any doubt that the eagle had driven the gimmer in between the rocks, as I could see by the state of the ground that she had been fixed there only a short time."

CHAPTER 15

THE COUNTRY OF THE EAGLE

A HIGH CORRIE OF THE CAIRNGORMS: GARBH CHOIRE MOR IN SPRING

"High aloft though he be, the fleet-footed hare escapeth not his ken, though he lurk
beneath a bosky thicket; but look! he swoops down upon it, and pouncing, at once robs
it of its life." – Homer's *Iliad*, book xvi.

In the heart of each lover of the wild places is a secret corrie of
the hills which he loves above all others. To my mind Garbh
Choire Mor (the Great Rough Corrie), where the Dee has its
birth, is the grandest of them all, and I have often wondered that
the golden eagle should not nest here (although, indeed, she is
constantly to be seen in the corrie). But then I have thought that it
would be difficult for an eagle to make her eyrie in the stupendous
cliffs of the Garbh Choire, because she nests early, and at the time
of her nesting the cliffs here are always deep in snow.

101

The Garbh Choire is enclosed on all sides by great hills, each of them more than 4000 feet in height. Eastwards Ben MacDhui intercepts the rays of the morning sun; south the cone of Cairntoul steeply rises; west and north the immense bulk of Brae Riach deflects the course of the winter storms. Thus Garbh Choire Mor is seen by few.

It is said that long ago a she-devil had her home in this wild corrie. It was she who gave to the Garbh Choire its first and now little-known name of Pit an Dheamhain, or the She-devil's Hollow, which is mentioned only once, I think, in print, and that is in an old book of still older records.

Well might the Garbh Choire have been thought the abode of a she-devil by primitive minds, who were inclined to look upon all hills with superstitious dread, especially when the wind made stern music amongst the cliffs. Below the precipices lie hundred upon hundred acres of granite boulders, which the people of olden times doubtless thought had been hurled from the hill-tops by the hand of the she-devil who lived in the corrie.

One can climb to Garbh Choire Mor by way of the Spey valley, crossing the Lairig and striking westward about a mile south of the Pools of Dee, or one can ascend Glen Dee from Mar.

The summer night on which a friend and I crossed from the Spey to Garbh Choire Mor was clear and calm after a day of showers. Brae Riach, the second highest of the Cairngorm range and the third highest hill in Britain, was bathed in a golden light of great beauty; even the sombre pines of its lower slopes shone as though afire. The western sky was serene and almost cloudless; eastward were many clouds and a few passing showers.

At ten o'clock the sun dipped below the horizon to the north-west, and for long the ruddy afterglow burned there.

In Lairig Ghru, supreme among Scottish passes, there was the silence of the high hills. The musical murmur of Allt na Criche seemed only to accentuate that silence, as did the occasional croaking of some ptarmigan.

Exactly at midnight we reached the crest of the pass where the Pools of Dee mirrored the pale stars. For some time the sky southward had shown us that the moon was rising behind Ben MacDhui, and now, at midnight, the golden orb climbed above the shoulder of that hill and lighted a pale fire in the dark pools that seemed to sleep.

The ptarmigan had gone to roost. The silence was intense. The full moon herself, shining mysteriously through a layer of thin clouds, seemed more serene and more full of wisdom than when viewed from the low grounds.

Through a land of great, solemn silence we walked south-ward until the mouth of the Garbh Choire was reached. A summer moon is low on the horizon always, and so to-night the moon climbed only a little way towards the zenith. But shining low, her beams caressed the swift-flowing waters of the young Dee, so that for miles southward down the glen they glowed as a sinuous line of fire.

In early summer the snows of the Garbh Choire are almost unbroken. The moon, from time to time obscured by drifting clouds, shone upon the south-facing snowy slopes of the corrie, and where she shone the snows were tinged faintly with gold which contrasted with the steel-grey snowy expanses that were in shadow.

In the faint moonlight the way up the Garbh Choire was testing, because the ground is peaty and the heather conceals the stones that form a trap for him who steps unwarily at dead of night. In a foaming torrent the infant Dee roared through the corrie. White as a bar of silver it shone in the darkness, and from Lochan Uaine of Cairntoul a second milky torrent leaped in a series of long cascades – a pale, indescribably beautiful streak against the black wall of rock. The corrie was filled with solemn music – the midnight music of the hills.

Once a hind barked sharply and hoarsely close to us, and a ptarmigan, suddenly aroused from sleep, flew off croaking. As we walked beside the grey line of the burn, full to the brim of snow-water, there was a sudden flutter of white wings and a hen ptarmigan rose from her nest. We examined the eggs by the light of a match – there were six of them, lying in a primitive unlined nest.

Beside the stream the dwarf juniper grows. Its green crowns were invisible, but the bleached stems of the old lifeless plants shone in the darkness white as the bones of some animal.

At last we reached the head of the corrie, where the snow lies summer and winter, as the first flush of dawn showed north-east. Westward, behind the black cliffs that enclose the corrie like an immense wall, the high floating *cirrus* clouds were tinged with lemon from a moon which was invisible to us behind the wall of rock. But when we climbed farther up we saw the moon herself, dimming her lamp against the dawn, and, sitting among the immense granite boulders, we awaited daylight.

All around us were great fields of snow, pale grey and mysterious. Up the rocky, steep slopes of Sgorr an Lochain Uaine opposite us a herd of phantom deer seemed to press eagerly, yet ever to remain in the same place. They appeared, to the unaided eye, to sway this way and that in confusion, but the glass showed that dark confused company as rocks rising above the snowy surface. The stars one by one disappeared, until at last there were but two that shone from the western sky.

A hundred yards below us a pair of ptarmigan were croaking as they awoke with the dawn. After a time the hen flew off down the hillside, perhaps to lay, while the cock, with a fluttering of white wings, ran up, flitting from boulder to boulder, towards us. He soon noticed us, and stood upon a boulder eyeing us suspiciously. As the light increased more ptarmigan crossed the hillside beneath us, and as they alighted to feed the still air was filled with their curious croaking notes.

At sunrise we had reached a lesser, and very beautiful, corrie of Garbh Choire Mor. This corrie is known as Garbh Choire Dhe, and is perhaps a mile north-east from the head of the main corrie, and divided from it by a wall of rocks. Its beauty is heightened because the Dee, from its source on the plateau of Brae Riach, leaps to it in a great waterfall and then flows quietly across the "floor" of the corrie.

There can be few more delightful places amid the high hills from which to watch the rising of the sun, and this morning in the clear soft air it seemed a fairy country.

Although the stream was in flood the waters were perfectly clear. There were quiet, gravelly pools in the corrie, and beside the burn, on banks that leaned steeply to the south, the cushion pink was opening its small pale pink blossoms.

Far eastward across Mar, and across the valley of the Dee beyond Braemar, the cone of Lochnagar rose against the sky, a deep purple bloom clothing its slopes. Already the sun was shining upon the snowfields that lay upon this hill of the Balmoral country, although on the Cairngorms the greyness of dawn lingered.

At length the sun reached Garbh Choire Mor, and the snows glistened and gleamed with intense, sudden light. The murmur of the Dee filled the corrie. The young river seemed to hurl itself with joy over the black precipice. Even on its course down the corrie it was partially imprisoned by the snow, and beneath the great waterfall flowed under a long snow bridge. The spray drifted far over the damp rocks; they glistened with moisture. In the air was that curious scent which lingers over a hill stream in spate.

Less than a week ago snow had lain unbrokenly in the corrie, but everywhere the alpine plants were growing vigorously. How wonderful is the sudden awakening from a prolonged sleep, such as hill plants sleep! In their young growth is a delightful and rare freshness, for the deeper and less disturbed the slumber the more joyous and vigorous the awakening.

Eastward, across a boulder-strewn spur, is another lesser corrie of Garbh Choire Mor. It is named Coire Bhrochain, or the Corrie of the Porridge, and, crossing the spur, we reached this corrie as the sun was climbing high.

The way to this corrie is across a wilderness of boulders and great rocks, lying as they were hurled in confusion by some cataclysm of nature thousands of years ago. In the shelter of one of these rocks bones were lying as though placed there by some animal. The bones were moss grown and apparently of a very great age: they seemed too large to belong to red deer – the only large animal one would have expected to find at that height – and they were later identified by an expert as the bones of cattle. It was extraordinary to find these bones at 3000 feet above sea-level, and the finding of them was of unusual interest, because it seemed to confirm a curious tradition which accounted for the naming of the corrie.

It is said that one day – it must have been at least a hundred years ago, and long before the Cairngorms became a deer forest in the present sense of the word – the cattle from one of the summer shielings in Glen Eanaich during a time of snow and thick mist lost their bearings and fell over the precipice that drops from the summit of Brae Riach to the corrie below. Their death must have been instantaneous, for when they were found they were crushed and mangled, and of the consistency of *brochan* or porridge. And so the name Coire Bhrochain, or Porridge Corrie, was given to that place.

There are few people now who believe in that old tradition, and I confess that I was sceptical of it myself. But the finding of those moss-covered bones seems to confirm the old legend that I first heard many years ago from Donald Fraser, the Mar stalker who lived at Derry Lodge and was so well known to all who climbed the Cairngorms.

A small tarn of clearest water is cradled in Coire Bhrochain, and this early summer morning the pool was surrounded by a glistening snowfield which had been piled up there by some winter storm. I remember being in the Corrie during one such storm and seeing a dark eagle soar past me in the teeth of the gale. The drifting snow was so cutting that I could with difficulty keep my head to the storm, and yet the eagle was soaring with no apparent discomfort in the very teeth of the blizzard.

From the floor of Coire Bhrochain one looks up a full eight hundred feet of sheer black cliff to the cairn that marks the top of Brae Riach, perched on the summit of the precipice. Seen even on a day of clear sky and bright sun this precipice is stern and grim. Picture what it must be when autumn storms sweep ragged armies of mist up its damp, glistening walls, and the gale makes wild music that seems to tell of striving between mountain and wind!

There is little soil in Coire Bhrochain even for hardy alpine plants. Stones, boulders, and great rocks lie everywhere, and thus few wild creatures have their home in the corrie. Perhaps a couple of pairs of ptarmigan may nest here, and one or two mountain hares, or an occasional meadow pipit may at times wander to its rocky slopes.

An avalanche must have swept over the precipice a short time before we entered the corrie, for in one place stones and boulders lay upon the surface of the snow, and stretched among the debris was a mountain hare, quite fresh, and showing on its head the gash which it must have received from some sharp rock during its swift drop to eternity.

How easy it is to visualise that tragedy of the high hills: the hare, feeding contentedly upon a grassy ledge on the young herbage, and in such a spot imagining itself secure from its enemies the hill fox and the eagle; the sudden breaking away of a snow cornice that, crashing down, overwhelmed the luckless hare and swept it, along with the plants on which it had been feeding, to the hard, unbroken snows that lay on the floor of the corrie far below!

It was September when next I looked into Garbh Choire Mor. The snows had gone, all but two small fields at the very head of the corrie. These fields have never been known to disappear, but they were then (September 1926) smaller than I had ever known them, and were so discoloured that it was hard to distinguish them from the surrounding hillside.

The clouds were grey in the corrie, but on the far distant-heights of Kintail, beside the Atlantic, there was sunshine, and a solitary eagle, steering swiftly north-west, passed from shade to sun, from dark to light, as he sailed beyond the black walls of Garbh Choire Mor.

CHAPTER 16

HIGHLAND STORIES OF THE EAGLE

Eagle and
Lambs

In another chapter I have mentioned that, in my opinion, an eagle becomes a lamb-eater in the same way that a lion becomes a man-eater. Few of those correspondents to whom I have written have seen an eagle take a living lamb, but the following persons have actually seen this, and I give their information as I received it.

John Grant, from Sluggan, Carr Bridge, Inverness-shire, writes as follows: "Some years ago I was a shepherd in Inverlaidnan Glen. About the first week of May, in the height of the lambing season, I was an eye-witness of the following: Along with another shepherd, about eight o'clock in the evening, we were attending to a ewe and a young lamb. We looked up and saw an eagle about two hundred yards from us. It circled round two or three times

108

and made a swoop down at a lamb. The mother of the lamb promptly rushed at the eagle and knocked it on its back in the heather. After recovering from the blow the eagle rose and flew away for about thirty yards, and dived down at another lamb and carried it away. The eagle rose in circles to a considerable height and flew along the slope of the hill. It gradually descended again, and when close to the ground lost hold of the lamb, which fell some fifteen or twenty feet into the heather.

"From the time the eagle attacked the first lamb and carried away the second we shouted and made the dogs bark, but the bird was so determined it did not heed us. When we got up to the lamb it was still alive, and able to run a little. It was bleeding on its right side from a nasty wound, and when we took it to its mother she refused to take it. We took the lamb home, but it was dead the next morning. We were sorry to lose it, as we should have liked to rear it after its unusual experience. The lamb was four days old, and a good specimen. I can vouch the above to be a perfect fact."

Robert Fraser writes as follows from Achnahyle, Tomintoul, Banffshire: "While on the hills a number of years ago I came round a sharp bend and saw an eagle about thirty feet in the air. It dropped something white, and on going to the spot I found a newly lambed black-faced wedder lamb, still alive, with a cut on one side. The ewe was some distance away. I brought the lamb to its mother, and it lived to be a wedder, although permanently disabled. This is the only case I have actually seen.

John G. MacKenzie writes from Dirdhu, Grantown-on-Spey: "On Sunday, 1st May 1910, my brother came upon an eagle in the act of carrying away a lamb from its mother's side. He shouted, and threw his stick at it. The eagle then dropped the lamb, which was cut on the throat and back. It had to be carried home and nursed for about a week before it was able to follow its mother. On the following Thursday the eagle carried another lamb fully one hundred and fifty yards from its mother's side; on my brother appearing the eagle rose from it. We have no proof that the eagle killed that lamb, but are fully convinced that it did, as we found that *both* sides had been cleaned by the mother. If the lamb had been born dead she would have cleaned only *one* side. Although to the best of my knowledge and belief the above statement is correct, I should be very sorry if it would be the cause of anyone trying to kill such a magnificent bird."

Duncan Robertson, west Inverness-shire, once saw an eagle rise clumsily, and on going to the spot found a dead lamb, quite warm, and with the marks of the eagle's talons in its neck.

Much the same thing was witnessed by Walter MacKay, a west Sutherland stalker. MacKay also saw an eagle lift a lamb from close beside its mother. The eagle rose with the lamb about two hundred feet, then let it drop. The only marks on the lamb were talon marks on the neck and head; one talon had pierced the brain.

Kenneth MacGregor, an east Sutherland keeper, writes: "I have seen personally an eagle swoop down on one of my own lambs and carry it three or four yards. When the ewe made a rush at the eagle she let the lamb go, and the ewe stood beside the lamb. When I reached the place the lamb was quite dead, for the eagle had put her claws through the body. This was a Cheviot lamb."

Duncan MacRae, Sutherlandshire, once saw about a dozen dead lambs on the rocks near an eagle's nest, but the lambs may have been dead when she carried them there.

While I think it is fair to quote in full the evidence against the eagle, it is right to point out that these letters represent only a small minority of the replies I have had. Most of my correspondents have never seen an eagle take a lamb, and surely the vividness with which shepherds and stalkers recall a single event of this kind shows what a rarity it must be. If eagles habitually took lambs we should hear very much more about it than we do.

A correspondent writes from the Hebrides: "A matter of twelve years ago a pair of golden eagles took heavy toll of black-faced lambs on the west side of the island. They worked together, one deliberately attracting the attention of, and irritating, the ewe, which usually charged and, rearing on its hind legs, struck at the eagle. Meantime the other swooped down behind and bore off the lamb. This was repeated practically daily over a considerable period, the eagles regularly succeeding in getting away with a lamb. Here, every year, there are golden eagles, but not every pair appears to think of attacking lambs. I may say that there are no rabbits here. Where there are rabbits the probability is that the eagles would pay no attention to lambs. I have observed the eyrie of golden eagles, with the eaglet only a few days hatched, full of the remains of the carcases of *rats*."

Hugh Stewart, west Inverness-shire, writes: "I have seen on one occasion an eagle swoop down on a lamb and carry it away. I watched him closely, and when very high up he dropped it for some reason, or it wriggled out of his clutches. Immediately he made another swoop and picked up another lamb. This time he flew a long way with the lamb and got out of view before landing. An observant shepherd told me that the eagle was a great worry to him, but he added that it did no damage after the end of June, when the lambs would be about 30 lb. live weight. I do not think an eagle ever attacks a full-grown sheep. It is my opinion that during the winter months the eagle lives chiefly on carrion, and does most of the destruction while rearing its young."

Another lamb story comes from D. MacRae from the west of Ross-shire: "I saw the eagle carrying a lamb just at the top of a high hill, I and another keeper being out fox-hunting. She flew straight overhead, and when we came into view suddenly she dropped a half-grown lamb almost at our feet. I would say the lamb would be 14 lb. It was quite warm, as if the eagle had just killed it. People maintain that they don't eat but what they kill, but this is a mistake. I have seen them eating off a dead carcase to the extent they could not fly. It was a dead calm day."

Ronald M'Coll, Argyllshire, tells me that one of his men saw the eagle swooping down on a three weeks' old lamb and carry it off, and that the same bird did this on four occasions, and he thinks the lambs would weigh from 12 to 20 lb.

It is curious that from upwards of sixty correspondents, all of whom have lived in the country of the eagle, I have heard of only about a dozen authentic instances of an eagle actually being seen to take living lambs. Yet these men are out on the hills daily and at all times of the year. The evidence that I have been able to collect seems to point to the fact that eagles probably take to lamb-killing only when food is scarce, and that with some eagles it becomes a habit. But they prey on lambs only during the first four weeks of their lives, while the eagles are rearing their own young. As it has been proved that eagles can actually kill deer even up to the age of a year, it follows that if they liked they could kill even a full-grown sheep, yet with one exception all the keepers and shepherds agree that they attack only young lambs. (In Chapter 14 I have quoted one instance of an eagle attacking a sheep wedged between two rocks.) Why do they not attack older sheep? It cannot

TEARING A ROE-DEER CALF — ABEL LOOKING ON ANXIOUSLY.

be a question of weight alone, for they could feed on the carcase where they killed it, as they undoubtedly do on large deer calves which they kill.

The conclusion is that sheep and lambs are really an unnatural prey of the eagle, taken only in exceptional circumstances, either because of scarcity of more natural food, or when peculiar conditions make it easy for the eagle to form the habit of preying on lambs. It is to the credit of the eagle that this should be so, when one thinks how easy a prey either a sheep or lamb must be in the hill country, where any white object can be seen for miles.

Eagles seem to take pleasure in alarming deer. I have more than once seen them swoop down close to a herd of grazing stags, causing the animals to shift their ground uneasily, and one of the very few times I have ever heard a golden eagle call was just after one of these playful "stoops" when his mate, sailing near, was watching him. *Eagle and Deer*

Charles Grant, head stalker in Mar Forest, tells me that once he saw two eagles in Glen Feshie swooping at a herd of hinds. He was hind-stalking at the time, and the combined attacks of the two eagles had made the herd so terrified, that Grant was able to walk up in full view of the hinds and shoot one of them at a distance of 100 yards!

Donald Urquhart, wester Ross-shire, once saw a hind driving an eagle away from her calf. The hind was standing on her hind feet and was striking out with her forefeet. Urquhart's brother once saw an eagle following a wounded stag, and he himself saw an eagle hover over a stag that had been hit and was lying down. The eagle settled close to the animal, but saw the stalkers approaching and flew away.

Several instances are on record of an eagle endeavouring to drive deer over a cliff by striking the animal with its great wings and causing it to rush forward blindly towards destruction.

Lochiel tells me that his late head stalker saw a pair of eagles pursuing and swooping at a herd of hinds and calves. Eventually the eagles separated a hind and a calf from the main herd and, buffeting the calf with their wings, drove it over the precipice toward which they had been endeavouring to herd the deer. The calf was killed by the fall and the eagles proceeded to devour it.

Major Ellice of Invergarry writes: "One day while spying I saw a large herd of stags and hinds driven straight past us at the gallop by an eagle. The eagle was trying to detach a deer calf – quite a large one – from the herd. I fired a couple of shots at the deer as they galloped past at about 200 yards, but missed them. The eagle never left his quarry, and when he was about a mile from us he succeeded in driving the calf away from the herd. He continued to swoop down upon it, and gradually drove it into a deep burn, where I suppose he finished it off." He continues: "Curiously enough, as we rose to go on with our stalk, a hare which had been lying within two yards of us, and unperceived, jumped up and rolled over dead. I suppose he died of fright."

F. Mackintosh, stalker in an Inverness-shire deer forest, in September 1925 saw three eagles attack a red deer calf. He writes: " I had just stalked and shot a stag out of a small mixed lot of stags and hinds, and was keeping the herd under observation with a view to getting another stag later on, when an eagle stooped on and struck a calf a terrific blow with her body. As far as I could see the eagle did not attempt to fix her talons or bill in the calf; she simply swooped down at a terrific pace, her wings folded and legs close up to her body. Scarcely had she ascended when another eagle attacked in the same manner, and then a third. All three birds adopted the same method of attack, and confined their attentions to the same animal. As it was September the calf was pretty well grown, and avoided a good many of the blows by wheeling sharply in little circles just as one of the big birds approached; but attack followed attack so quickly that he very soon got exhausted, and then one of the eagles fixed her talons in his withers and, flapping her huge wings savagely, bore the calf to the ground.

"At this stage the other two eagles alighted some few yards from the one that had just killed the calf, and did not seem to be in any hurry to join the feast. Meantime the herd had moved on a considerable distance, and never paid any attention to the tragedy that was happening to one of their number. Had the deer not been fired at some time before they would have closed in, and prevented the eagles driving one of their number out of the herd."

John MacDonald, head stalker in a west Inverness-shire forest, tells me that he has often seen the eagle scattering deer in all directions. He once saw an eagle chase a hind into a deep gorge, hoping evidently to kill it, but the eagle was disturbed by seeing him. The eagle's method of attack was to swoop past the deer for some distance, and then, turning abruptly, to fly back and strike the animal in the face.

James Davidson, stalker in Inverness-shire, writes: " I have frequently seen an eagle stoop and fix his claws on the back of a six-quarter-old deer, which would gallop up to its mother, when the eagle would at once quit his hold and sheer off. I have often seen a hind defending her calf from an eagle, but I have never actually seen a fight; the eagle knows better than to get within range of an old hind's forefeet."

Andrew MacKay, a Sutherland stalker, in February saw two eagles circling low about some deer on the high ground. The eagles singled out a young deer and chased the animal over the skyline out of his sight.

Many stalkers have seen the eagle chase deer calves, but almost always the mothers, or the herd, have checked the attack.

Charles Mackintosh, for many years second stalker on the Balmoral Forest, once saw an eagle killing a red deer calf in the month of July with beak and talons, while the luckless calf screamed like a baby. Andrew MacKay, quoted above, once saw an eagle lift a red deer calf high in the air and then let it drop. The bird did not go near it again.

James MacDonald, Inverness-shire, also saw an eagle lift a deer calf off the ground, but the bird did not get away with its quarry because the mother hind and a number of other hinds "practically fought the eagle, and eventually the mother hind stood over the calf with the others gathered around in a group."

Mr R. MacMorran, Isle of Mull, tells me that there is a tradition that an eagle carried a deer calf from the Isle of Scarba across the sea to the high sea-cliffs of Carsaig, Isle of Mull, a distance of at least eight miles.

Major Ellice of Invergarry writes: "In the late autumn of 1926 I was walking in line on the extreme right, trying to get one or two grouse – four guns – a vile day with snow showers. A deer calf suddenly came quite close to me, and followed me so close that I could put out my hand to him to try to entice him to be friendly. After walking for about half a mile (the calf always keeping his place on the right flank) we caught up with a herd of deer on the face of a hill south of us. The calf also spotted them and trotted off to the herd. An eagle at once appeared from nowhere and attacked the calf, but fortunately the herd was too big and the calf joined up."

James Grant, at one time stalker in the Invercauld Forest, tells me that once in Glen Callater he saw an eagle driving a three-month-old deer calf down a very steep hillside. The eagle was stooping repeatedly, and every time he struck the calf it yelled with pain and fright. Grant could not follow them, but thinks it almost certain that the eagle finished off the calf. The herd of deer from which the calf had been detached was feeding about a mile away.

Duncan MacRae, Sutherlandshire, saw an eagle tackle a well-grown deer calf in the month of February, fixing his talons in the animal's back and flapping his wings in its eyes. The calf galloped downhill to the herd, and the herd at once drove off the aggressor.

Æneas Cameron, Ross-shire, tells me that he has seen an eagle trying to drive a hind over a rock, and would have succeeded had not the hind got into a burn. He also came on a pair of eagles killing a one-year-old stag. It was not quite dead when he came upon them, but he says "they had the skin and flesh holed on the ribs." This instance is remarkable, and it looks as if this young stag must have been alone or perhaps unhealthy. This is the only instance I know of so old a deer being killed by eagles.

Donald Mackintosh, central Ross-shire, writes that he has seen an eagle chasing deer and alighting on the shoulders of a six-quarter-old hind, but an older hind, probably the mother of the young hind, galloped up to her rescue.

Murdoch Macdonald, central Ross-shire, once found an eagle on a newly killed deer fawn about six weeks old. It was holed behind the shoulder and a good bit of it had been eaten, and as the skin was a pretty one he skinned the calf, and found that it had been killed by the eagle's talons piercing right through its skull. On another occasion he saw an eagle chasing a hind. "The hind got into a hole below a rock and the eagle perched close above it." He watched it for quite an hour. "The hind would sometimes come out a little way and look whether the eagle was still there and then go in again. But the eagle was never moving. At last it flew away and went right out of sight. Directly the eagle went out of sight the hind galloped along the side of the hill, but she wasn't 200 yards away when the eagle was back again and attacked it; but the hind got into another cave and the eagle perched again as close to it as it could get. We watched them for another half-hour and left them in that position, so I can't say what the sequel was, but the eagle was quite determined on killing it."

James MacLean writes to me: "I was out stalking, and I noticed the eagle coming across from Meoble Forest and attacking a herd of deer. She swooped round the herd several times, and you could hear her *bark* quite distinctly. At last she attacked one of the hinds by resting on its withers and pecking its neck. This hind then broke away from the rest of the herd, and in its headlong gallop went over the 200-feet cliff that was near. The eagle did not come immediately to the dead hind, but sailed round the corrie for awhile. She then came back and rested on a rock immediately above where the carcase lay, and after resting for a short time flew down to feed on it. I feel sure eagles drive deer in any direction they wish, just as a dog would do.

"On another occasion I noticed an eagle flying low over a clump of bracken. After swooping several times into the bracken she put out a fawn, which she attacked. The mother hind was lying farther up the hill, and when she heard the fawn bleating she came galloping down and chased the eagle, which was now flying about six feet from the ground. But her efforts to save her young were hopeless, for the eagle lifted the fawn three times off the ground to a height of about forty to fifty feet, and each time let it drop so that it was killed by the fall."

Another stalker on one occasion saw a golden eagle on the back of a full-grown deer. The deer was travelling at great speed, the eagle all the while flapping her wings. She was seen to urge her terrified steed forward for at least two miles, but then eagle and deer were lost to view.

John MacDonald writes: "I once saw an eagle swoop down on a herd of deer in Corrour Forest. She picked up a calf about three weeks old and carried it to the top of a high boulder about two hundred yards away. The whole herd of hinds followed the eagle. They surrounded the boulder, bleating and making a fearful din. The eagle sat like a statue admiring the whole scene for the matter of ten minutes, then started feeding on her capture.

The Hon. Alastair Fraser writes as follows to me: "About 1898 or '99, in Glendoe Forest, I saw the following incident. The stalker and I heard a rattle of stones from across the glen, and saw a hind and calf picking their way across a steep scree of loose shaly rock. We then saw that an eagle was attacking them. The bird repeatedly swooped down on the pair, but never as far as we could see attempted to strike them. Each time the bird came close, the hind stood stock-still and the calf disappeared under her belly. The moment the danger was passed the hind walked gingerly on, the calf following close behind. These tactics were repeated a dozen times to the best of my recollection. As soon as the hind got on to solid ground the pair cantered off and the eagle left them. It seemed to us that had the hind lost her head, the calf at any rate would have lost its footing even if she had not. As far as I can recollect there was a fall of over 100 feet (at the angle of rest for this shaly stuff), and a fall must have resulted in broken legs. The stalker told me that a man could not cross the line the deer took, or at any rate he would not try. As far as I recollect we watched the deer for about 100 yards across it. When we first saw them they were, I think, about the middle of the scree. How or why the hind and calf got themselves into this difficult position we could not tell."

Another correspondent who has actually seen an eagle drive a deer over a cliff is Alick Whamond. He writes: "One January day I saw an eagle swooping down on a hind in very poor condition. It started driving the hind towards the rocks. When the beast tried to turn, the eagle flew at it and struck it with its wings till it got it to go the right way. At last the hind fell over the cliff and the eagle made a good meal of it. The snow had been lying on the ground for a long time, and I think the eagle must have been driven to attack the hind through hunger."

Donald Ross, stalker in a western forest, writes: "One day, on coming round a bend in a forest path, I was surprised to see about fifteen hinds within 100 yards of me, all gathered together in a bunch with their tongues out. I could hear them breathing from where I stood. I looked up the hillside, and there I saw a young hind galloping away with an eagle fixed on her back. Sometimes the eagle would rise in the air a few feet, then it would fix on again and keep flapping its wings against the hind. They finally disappeared over the edge of a very steep and rocky hill, and I am almost certain that the hind was bound to get killed among the rocks."

I have few records of encounters between roe-deer and eagle. Eagle and Mr. Robert Hargreaves, of the Forest of Gaick, tells me that he Roe-deer once saw a roebuck attacked by an eagle. The plucky roe showed no signs of fear, but rose on his hind legs and struck out at the surprised eagle with his forelegs, when the eagle made off. On another occasion a roebuck was attacked in Glen Feshie. The buck was feeding at the edge of a birch wood when an eagle suddenly swooped and struck at the roe, who dodged the blow and bounded for the nearest clump of trees, where he continued to graze unconcernedly. The eagle did not renew the attack.

John Don, Inverness-shire, once saw an eagle on a roe-deer's back, and, he says, "if the roe-deer had not got into a thick wood I am quite sure the eagle would have killed that roe-deer."

Roe-deer keep usually to the woods, and as they are screened by the trees the eagle sees them less frequently than red deer, but, as I have mentioned in another chapter, roe calves are sometimes taken by the eagle to its eyrie.

CHAPTER 17

HIGHLAND STORIES OF THE EAGLE

FOXES AND CATS

"The captive thrush may brook the cage,
The prison'd eagle dies for rage. "– Scott , *Lady of the Lake*.

Eagle and Fox

Once, on the plateau of Beinn A'an, I saw the fur and skin of a fox scattered over the ground, and I have little doubt that an eagle, coming upon a fox (perhaps a young animal) unawares, had killed it and made a meal of it there and then.

I have received a number of interesting accounts of fights, or "sparring matches," between fox and eagle. Old John Ferguson, a native of Badenoch and a stalker of many years' experience, told me that on one occasion he approached unobserved an eagle's eyrie in a rock. He noticed that a fox was half-way down the rock,

120

attracted by the ptarmigan in the eyrie (Ferguson could see their white wings). Overhead the two parent eagles were soaring.

The fox soon saw that he could not reach the "larder," and evidently did not think the spot a healthy one with the old eagles so close. He climbed the rock and trotted off across the moor, and as he went he held his brush straight up in the air. Ferguson thinks he did this in order that, as he put it, "better his tail should be attacked than he himself."

On another occasion Ferguson was out stalking with a gentleman. They were near the top of a hill when the stalker saw what he thought was the antler of a stag in "velvet" crossing the skyline. Ferguson was afraid that they had disturbed the deer which he knew were ahead of them, and kept very still. But the fancied stag in "velvet" was only a fox. An eagle was soaring close above him, and this fox also was holding his brush straight in the air, since the eagle was too near for his liking. The supposed antler in "velvet" was the fox's brush!

One day, when Ferguson was visiting his traps in Glen Feshie, he came to where he had set a trap on either side of a "bait," and found a golden eagle in one trap and a fox in the other. Ferguson tells me that the best method of trapping a fox is by setting two traps, because if a fox is at all suspicious of a "bait" he waits until he sees that something is caught. For example, when he sees a hooded crow struggling in a trap the wily old fox thinks to himself, "Now that the trap has caught somebody it cannot catch me," and then walks up and eats his fill. Thus it is necessary for the trapper to match cunning with cunning. On this occasion Ferguson believes the fox must have seen the eagle trapped, and, chuckling to himself, came in on the other side – and was caught too! The eagle was alive, but very weak because of its long imprisonment in the trap. The trap had been set for a fox, and Ferguson told me he was more than sorry to find an eagle in it. He carried the great bird home, and kept it for some time in a shed, hoping it would recover. In a few days it became so tame that it would allow the stalker to open its bill and push small pieces of venison down its throat; unfortunately it did not long survive.

Sometimes fox and eagle feed together off a dead deer, and a stalker told me that once during a bad snowstorm he spied a fox and eagle eating a carrion deer and, stalking them, shot the fox.

THE FOUR EAGLES AT THE NEST TOGETHER. THE COCK HAS BROUGHT A STICK, THE HEN IS LOOKING OUT OVER THE CORRIE.

Major Ellice of Invergarry tells me that he once saw a fox and an eagle, one on each side of a small "nobber," watching a dead hare. Peter Stewart, Perthshire, once saw an eagle giving chase to a fox. Time after time the eagle swooped down and, in passing, slashed at the fox with its wing. The fox showed no fight, but flopped down flat on the ground each time to escape the blow. The pursuit continued for nearly a mile, when the fox got to ground in some deep moss hags. Then the eagle flew back and, alighting where the fox had first appeared, commenced to feed on the carcase of a deer.

The same stalker saw a raven summarily executed by an eagle. Some ravens were feeding in the snow on a dead sheep. An eagle appeared and, as the ravens were rising from the ground, swooped down and seized a large raven with its talons. The eagle alighted, dropped the raven beside the carcase and commenced to feed on the sheep. The raven was quite dead, having been pierced through the body.

David Dempster, West Perthshire, tells me that he once saw an interesting trial of strength between eagle and fox. He was out stalking, and says: "We got up to beasts, and found that our stag lay down. So we decided to wait until he got up. When we were waiting an eagle came and sat upon a big flat rock about fifty yards from us. We could see by the bird's movements that he was in a bad temper, and annoyed by something lower down the bill, as he kept twisting and turning his head and craning his neck. A fox came into sight about thirty yards lower down and came stalking up a hollow towards the eagle. He kept rather to the right of the eagle until he got above him, then he moved slowly towards the eagle, just like a dog 'drawing' on birds. When about a yard from the eagle the fox stood with tail straight out, one leg up, like a dog on grouse, and the eagle faced him with neck stretched forward. In this position they faced each other for some little time, then the fox drew himself up, arched his back, and made a spring for the eagle, who was ready for him and, as I thought, met the fox half-way, slashing at the fox with wings and talons. The fox had to run, the eagle slashing him as he went. It was all over in a very short time, the fox running downhill while his friend sailed about quite proud of himself, as we thought. My gentleman did not get a shot at that stag, as the deer cleared out while the scrap was going on, but it was well worth while losing a shot for that wonderful sight we had seen. I can still see that picture, although it is just thirty years since it happened."

Duncan MacRae, Sutherland, once saw a fox galloping up a hill near him. When he was about eighty yards off an eagle suddenly came up behind him, caught him, lifted him about a yard off the ground, then dropped him. The fox turned round to keep the eagle off, and the two stared at each other, the fox with his mouth open showing his teeth and the eagle with his neck out and his feathers ruffled. The fox then tried to make off, but the eagle soon caught him and lifted him about a dozen feet off the ground this time. Again he dropped the fox, and again on the ground the same staring match took place. The fox then made off and the eagle pursued, but did not lift him this time. The fox was a big dog-fox, and must have proved a heavy weight for the eagle.

James Davidson, keeper in Inverness-shire, writes: "I saw an eagle attack a fox one day on the hill. The fox got up on its hind legs open-mouthed and bit and snapped all round, and while the eagle was rising to make another stoop the fox made off as hard as he could gallop. When the eagle stooped at him again he stood up on his hind legs as before and snapped and bit at him, and before the eagle could stoop again the fox had reached some haggy ground where the eagle could not get at him."

Alex. MacDonald, west Inverness-shire, writes: "I once saw an eagle chase a fox, and every time the eagle would try to catch the fox he would turn on her. Before the eagle finished chasing the fox she caught him by the hind quarters and lifted him about ten or fifteen yards in the air; the fox turned and caught the eagle by the breast and she was obliged to let him go."

From Murdoch Macdonald, central Ross-shire, comes the following story: "A keeper friend of mine was watching a fox den, and he had a fox cub tied to a stake below the cairn to entice the old fox to come so that he could shoot her. Suddenly he heard the bleat of a lamb above him, and when he looked up he saw an eagle with a lamb in its talons. It passed directly above the cub, and hesitated as though looking at it. He knew where the eyrie was about a mile away, and watched the eagle go straight to it, and in a few minutes it was back again for the fox cub. The next act I won't mention," concludes this interesting tale.

M. Matheson, Inverness-shire, writes that on one occasion a fox trap with six-inch jaw, with chain weight 4 lb., and a three-foot pin, one inch across, sunk in peaty ground, was carried complete by an eagle a distance of three miles, and found with the corpse of the eagle fixed in a tree.

Donald Crerar, head stalker on Ardverikie Forest and a direct descendant of the Crerar mentioned in Scrope's classic work on Deer Stalking, has given me the following vivid narrative of a fight between a golden eagle and a wild cat: *Eagle and Cat*

With Sir John Ramsden's two sons, Crerar was on a fishing expedition in the forest in June 1924. He was on the shore of the loch when he noticed that a golden eagle was swooping, time after time, towards a steep rocky hill-face about 700 yards away. At first no particular attention was paid to the bird, but as it continued to swoop Crerar put the glass on it and followed its dive. He saw an animal sitting on a rounded stone upon a ledge of rock, and it was at this animal that the eagle kept stooping.

At first Crerar thought the beast was a red deer fawn, and then he thought that it must be a fox that had been rolling itself in peat, because its coat seemed to be darker than the coat of a fox should have been. But when at last the animal sprang into the air, striking at the eagle with its paws, Crerar saw that it was a wild cat. Time after time the eagle swooped down upon the cat, with its talons ready to grasp it and its strong legs outstretched. Once, as it came very near, the wild cat again sprang into the air, striking at the eagle with its claws. The spring was such a great one that Crerar distinctly saw the whole of the cat momentarily suspended in mid-air.

This must have alarmed the eagle, as it did not venture quite so near again. Altogether the eagle swooped at the wildcat thirty or forty times, but the cat sprang up at the eagle twice only. At last the wild cat disappeared into a cranny amongst the stones and the eagle sailed away.

A few days later Crerar climbed to the ledge of rock and found that the wild cat had her den there. It was curious that the wild cat should have thus exposed herself to the attacks of the eagle, because, so far as Crerar could see, the kittens were not out in the open.

The golden eagle is fond of tame cats, and no doubt it would be only too glad to make a meal off a wild cat did it not respect those sharp claws.

A pair of eagles which formerly had their eyrie on one of the Outer Hebrides used to hunt the cats of the island which had run wild and prowled over the moors, and used to take them to the eyrie for the eaglets. As the wild cat is now on the increase in the Highlands, it is possible that the eagle may, from time to time, take one of these fierce animals unawares and bear it to the nest.

Murdoch MacDonald, head stalker on a well-known Ross-shire deer forest, found traces of a more sanguinary fight between eagle and wild cat. He writes: "It happened not more than half a mile from my own house two years ago. There had been a heavy fall of snow through the night and in the early morning, and when I went out I found a wild cat's track quite near the house, so I got my gun and terrier and followed it. The track went along a steep slope where there was no other mark in the snow. I noticed where I thought the cat must have caught a grouse or something, as there were feathers and apparently the marks of a struggle in the snow. But when I reached the spot and examined the feathers I knew they were the head- and neck-feathers of an eagle. Then I saw that instead of the cat having caught something, as I had first thought, he had been caught himself. I could distinctly see the marks of the eagle's wings on the snow where it had come down on the cat, but seemingly the cat had been too quick, and must have caught the eagle by the head, for both had rolled down the steep slope for about thirty yards, where there was a little dip in the slope. There they had had a further struggle, for there were more feathers and a few drops of blood. When the combatants separated the cat must have been dazed, for he kept going round and round in circles in the snow before he got his bearings. But he went another half-mile before I got him in a cairn."

An interesting sequel to this fight was the finding on Blaven, in Skye, of a dead eagle a short time later. A lifeless eagle lying out on the hill is a rare thing to see, and this eagle had been severely injured about the neck and had apparently succumbed to its injuries. It would seem probable, therefore, that this was the same bird that had been mauled by the wild cat on the mainland some distance away (see Chapter 22).

CHAPTER 18

HIGHLAND STORIES OF THE EAGLE

GROUSE, GOOSE, PEREGRINE AND OTHER VICTIMS

Perhaps the most interesting thing in the letters I have received Eagle and from many correspondents on this subject is the fact that Grouse hardly any of the observers have ever seen an eagle actually take a grouse on the wing or on the ground. Now, when it is considered that the eagle does habitually prey upon grouse, that seems to me to be a very remarkable thing.

James Davidson, Inverness-shire, tells me that never during his forty years' experience of eagles and grouse has he seen an eagle take a grouse on the wing, and only once has he seen an eagle make a determined attempt to do so. On that occasion the eagle chased the grouse for half a mile, and would have caught its prey in another couple of yards had the grouse not bumped into a six-foot wire-netting run which Davidson had for puppies near his door. The grouse was killed by the blow; the eagle missed the netting by inches.

On another occasion an eagle, perhaps the same bird, made, writes Davidson, "a sudden stoop at a big white Aylesbury drake my wife had. The drake was puddling in a pool of water within twenty yards of the door. I saw an eagle circling about on top of a hill a mile off, and while I looked the eagle suddenly closed its wings and stooped straight for our place. I could hear the noise of it coming through the air like a whirlwind. It made straight for the drake and only just missed him."

Truly a thrilling sight, and one that could not have been described more graphically.

Two Sutherland stalkers, J. Brydon and Andrew MacKay, have given me accounts of how they saw a grouse taken by an eagle on the wing. Brydon writes: "The eagle came flying slowly, and what one would term tacked the top side of the hill first, then turned back and did the same thing say about half-way down. It put up three grouse, which kept together for some time but separated as the eagle got nearer to them. The eagle singled out a grouse and made after it, and in a few seconds made up on the grouse. After a few twists in the air, the eagle sometimes under the grouse and other times above it, the grouse shot straight for the ground. The eagle then like lightning swooped straight down past the grouse, turned back, met the falling grouse, shot out its left leg, and caught the grouse roughly fifty yards from the ground."

Andrew MacKay writes: "I was on high ground on the side of a corrie spying about and nine grouse passed hard on the wing. In a short time another two came and the eagle almost in line with them. When they went down the corrie the eagle was a little in front of the grouse, and as the grouse turned the eagle took one of them about ten feet from the ground."

Only two stalkers of the many I have met or corresponded with have seen a ptarmigan taken on the wing by an eagle.

John Ferguson tells me he has seen this more than once in the high corries of the western Cairngorms. He said that a breeze was necessary for the eagle to do this, and that in windy weather when a covey of ptarmigan rose and flew across from one side of the corrie to the other the eagle would easily overhaul them, and without any fuss take one of the birds in its foot and fly off with it.

STRIKING A GREY LAG.

Donald MacIver, Isle of Skye, tells me that he once saw an eagle seize and carry off an old blackcock in the air.

Although I have watched the golden eagle on very many occasions I have never seen it take a grouse or ptarmigan, but one autumn day, when in a lonely glen in the Forest of Mar, I saw an eagle pass overhead carrying a grouse. The bird must have been picked up very recently, for it was still alive, and from time to time flapped one wing helplessly. The eagle for a while circled around, then alighted upon the hillside and proceeded to make a meal of its unfortunate victim.

The following story from Murdoch Macdonald, central Ross-shire, is, I think, unique: "One very fine day, when I was in the act of setting a fox-trap, about the end of October, I observed two eagles coming in my direction pursuing a grouse. They were quite half a mile away when I noticed them. One eagle would be about forty yards behind the other from the time I saw them till the finish of the chase. The grouse was going at a great pace, but I could see the eagle was steadily gaining. When they were about three hundred yards away from and opposite me - the eagle was hardly moving her wings but was cutting along like a knife, and when she was within a yard of the grouse she suddenly drew in her wings, the tips of her wings close to her body, and shot forward like a ball – I distinctly heard the thump when she struck the grouse. There was a cloud of feathers and it dropped. What I wondered at was that she never stopped or altered her course, but the following eagle picked the grouse up and carried on after his mate, and disappeared over the edge of the hill. I am quite positive this eagle struck the grouse with her breast or shoulder – I mean by shoulder the front joint of the wing when not extended."

This is believed by some observers to be the way the peregrine falcon kills its prey on the wing, but of course the eagle usually kills its prey on the ground with its talons, and as my other correspondents who saw an eagle take grouse on the wing are positive that the bird was seized in the eagle's talons and not struck down, the above story is of exceptional interest.

Eagle and Goose — Very few persons have seen an eagle "bind to" a goose, but Walter MacKay, Sutherland, was fortunate enough to see this while stalking on Scourie in September 1915. He writes: "From forty to fifty geese were flying at a height of probably 1000 feet, when I saw them suddenly change their direction, at the same time making a great noise. On putting my telescope on them I could see an eagle following them, and on getting above them he settled down on one of them about the centre of the flock, and I felt certain that he fixed his talons in this goose, as they dropped straight down, and all the time he appeared to have hold of the goose. They dropped on some dead ground about half a mile from me and over my 'march,' and so I could not go to them."

Mr Robert MacMorran, of Treshnish, Mull, once saw an eagle rob a peregrine of its prey, and writes to me as follows: "A Locbuie keeper fishing near Loch Sguaban noticed a peregrine, which had its eyrie in the big rock above Creag, flying across from Ben Add with something in its claws. When the falcon was about half-way across two eagles came on the scene at a lower altitude, giving chase. The falcon made strenuous efforts to escape, but eventually had to drop its burden, which fell amongst the heather on the hillside at no great distance from the keeper. Both eagles gave up pursuit of the peregrine and tried to find the booty, hovering over the spot for a long time. The keeper ultimately went up and found, not a grouse as he expected, but a grey crow!" *Eagle and Peregrine*

Mr Alfred MacAulay, Golspie, a keen observer, writes: "The fight in the air I witnessed between eagle and peregrine falcon was, I think, in June 1894. A friend and I were fishing Loch Lundie between here and The Mound. Coming home in the afternoon we saw an eagle get up quite near us, and at that moment out came a peregrine falcon from the Silver Rock, steadied himself over the eagle and came down like a bolt. Just as we thought he was likely to strike the eagle the latter turned right over – a 'cart wheel' – and we saw him reach out his feet and claws for the peregrine, but the peregrine was up again. The eagle righted himself, and in a little down came the peregrine again, and the eagle again performed the 'cart wheel'. This was done five or six times, then the peregrine went off and the eagle flew round by The Mound Rock. It was a magnificent sight."

As I have mentioned elsewhere, the prey of the golden eagle consists mainly of mountain hares, rabbits, grouse, or ptarmigan, with an occasional lamb, red deer calf, roe-deer calf, and squirrel. *The Prey of the Eagle*

I have asked a number of stalkers and keepers to tell me of any unusual prey that they have known the eagle take, and I give below some of their replies.

John MacLeod, keeper, Isle of Skye, writes that he has seen a grey crow and a rook in the eyrie, and that one day, on the high moors, he came upon an eagle eating a stoat. The stoat was newly killed, for its blood was quite warm.

I myself have seen a stoat in an eagle's eyrie, and it is not so long ago that a stalker in the north of Scotland saw a golden eagle rise high in the air then suddenly fall to the earth. He ran up, and from where the eagle lay a stoat appeared and ran off. There was a deep bite in the eagle's throat, and there seemed no doubt that the eagle had picked the stoat up, meaning to make a meal of it, and that the stoat had succeeded in fastening its teeth in the eagle's neck. The eagle had risen hoping to shake off its small adversary, but the stoat had clung grimly and at last had brought the eagle down.

Donald MacIver, keeper in the Isle of Skye, once found a very small collie dog, almost as small as a Cairn terrier, in an eagle's nest. It is possible that the dog was caught in a trap, or dead when taken by the eagle.

Charles Mackintosh, Aberdeenshire, saw at one time at an eyrie a greyhen, a weasel, a black water-vole, and two grouse. At another time Mackintosh saw an eagle feeding on a magpie.

D. Mackintosh, central Inverness-shire, once saw a salmon in an eagle's eyrie. There were a few bites out of the salmon's shoulder, pointing to the fact that an otter had killed the fish and left it on the river bank. It is possible, however, that the golden eagle does at times take fish, for John MacLeod (whom I have quoted previously) tells me that once at the mouth of Loch Kishorn he saw a golden eagle swoop down and take a fish from a cormorant on the water. This of course sounds as though it were the work of the sea – and not the golden eagle, but MacLeod was convinced that the bird he saw was a golden eagle.

Walter MacKay saw a heron in the eyrie on two occasions, and he has also seen fox cubs at an eagle's nest.

M. Matheson, west Inverness-shire, has also seen fox cubs at an eyrie, but he knew they had been taken dead, as they had had their tails removed by some foxhunter. He has also seen seagulls at an eyrie, and once a pike, evidently killed by something else.

The finding of a salmon and a pike is interesting, because Cameron, head keeper at Inveraray, never succeeded in coaxing his captive young eagle to take morsels of fish.

Duncan Robertson, west Inverness-shire, once found in an eyrie a small egg, resembling the egg of a pheasant; and J. Brydon, a Sutherland stalker, has seen green and golden plover and moles at an eagle's nest. The finding of moles is most unusual and interesting, but Brydon writes that on hot sunny days he has frequently seen moles running on the surface of the green grass, and that at such times they are caught by birds of prey.

Mr R. MacMorran, Isle of Mull, has seen a raven and a cat in an eagle's eyrie. He tells me that on two occasions an eagle attacked one of his cats quite close to the farmhouse, but was unsuccessful both times.

An Inverness-shire keeper writes: "The first time I went to the eyrie there were five grouse in the nest, beautifully dressed – no kitchen-maid could handle them better just ready for the roasting-pan – also a fine old blackcock. The day before the eaglets flew there were two well-grown leverets in the nest without one single hair on them. They were whole-skinned, but it has always been a mystery to me how the eagles got the hair off them. This nest was kept scrupulously clean, not a bone or even a casting to be seen, and about every week the nest was relined with leaves from a sort of mountain willow."

The same keeper writes: "Once when fox-hunting in the spring of the year an eagle stooped at our terriers, and we had to run at our hardest, and even shoot at the eagle, to keep it off till such time as we got hold of the terriers. The terrier which, in my opinion, drew the eagle was an old favourite straw-coloured Dandy Dinmont, easily seen.

An eagle also attacked a Cairn terrier belonging to Donald MacDougall, an Inverness-shire stalker, swooping twice at it but fortunately missing it on each occasion.

CHAPTER 19

HIGHLAND STORIES OF THE EAGLE

The Strength of the Eagle The weight an eagle can carry must necessarily depend on the power of its wings rather than on the strength of its legs, but the following incident related by Robert Burns, central Ross-shire, demonstrates the enormous strength of an eagle's legs: "I was on the hill visiting fox-traps, and in one particular place I found that an eagle had been caught. Two traps had been set to this bait and pegged in such a way that they could not be moved out of the position they were in. The eagle had got his two feet caught, one in each trap. In one of the traps a toe was left, the S of the chain of the other trap was pulled almost straight out, and the eagle and trap were away. I had examined the chains before setting, and they were fit for any fox, especially as they were in water. Later on this bird was found alive and my trap still

134

on the foot – the distance was five miles away, and thirty days afterwards. On another occasion an eagle went away with one of my traps, as the ring of the chain had burst in the water. About a fortnight afterwards I was sitting in the same corrie when I spotted an eagle hunting towards me and carrying something. With the aid of the glass I could make out my trap and chain swinging about with the movements of the bird, which did not appear to be the least handicapped, as it was hunting in real earnest. Like the other eagle it was found later, though not alive."

There has always been much controversy over the weight lifting powers of the eagle. It is proved beyond doubt that eagles can lift new-born lambs, and, as I have mentioned elsewhere, it is believed to take lambs three weeks old. Thus it seems certain that the bird is able to lift from 9 to 11 lb. at least off the ground. A stalker of my acquaintance once saw an eagle going to the eyrie early in August with a red deer calf, head and all. The eagle passed close to him, and he estimates that the deer calf, from its size, must have weighed at least 20 lb. I admit this evidence is largely conjecture, but the average deer calf is some eight weeks old in August, and thus is of considerable weight.

Mr MacMorran, Isle of Mull, writes: "I have noticed that the eagle often drops its prey after rising to a considerable height with it. On each occasion the hare it dropped was struggling violently and screaming. I have noticed that the eagle usually came down and picked up the dead body. On one occasion she did not bother to do this, and I went over and took the hare. On steep ground the hare gives the eagle no trouble to lift, but on a calm day, or on level ground, she has difficulty in rising if she has anything to carry."

John MacLeod, Skye, writes: "In 1906 I found an eagle with a large trap, which would be about 8 lb. weight, hanging to one of his talons. I knew all the traps in use in Sleat (where the eagle was found), and there was none of that kind in the parish.

"The eagle must have come either from the Isle of Rhum or from the Cuillin Hills, at least twelve miles across the sea. I took the eagle home, and had him for about three months. I used to tether him, and however well and cunningly I would tie the knots on a cord on his leg, he would have them undone with his beak as soon as I would turn my back.

THE GOLDEN EAGLE BRINGS A HEATHER BRANCH TO THE EYRIE — NOTE THE THIRD EYELID IS DRAWN OVER THE EYE.

"I have seen an eagle straighten out the hook which attached the chain to a trap. I could not make that hook straight, and our gardener here, who has very strong hands, could not make the hook straight, so the eagle's strength is enormous."

For a golden eagle to fly twelve miles over the sea with an 8lb. trap hanging from its leg, and doubtless paining it all the time, is a remarkable testimony to its strength and endurance.

Robert Burns, Ross-shire, and Kenneth Sinclair, Inverness-shire, have both watched a golden eagle playing with a rabbit. The eagle observed by Sinclair never succeeded in catching the rabbit before it reached the ground. Burns, on the other hand, writes: "She was dropping a partly eaten rabbit, turning a sort of half-somersault and catching it again before it would drop many yards." *The Eagle at Play*

Duncan MacRae writes: "There was about a foot of snow on the ground. Hares were fairly numerous. I put up a few, and a golden eagle crossed the hillside, lifted three of the hares a few feet off the ground, and then dropped them. The hares 'carried on,' apparently none the worse!"

Donald Fraser, Mar, told me that once while he was "greallaching" a deer beside the Derry Water he heard a splash close to him. He looked up quickly and saw a golden eagle only a few yards above him. The eagle had evidently been playing with a ptarmigan, which it had dropped into the burn, and on seeing Fraser had become alarmed and had failed to bring off its catch.

James Davidson, Inverness-shire, writes: "One day I saw two eagles soaring together in the sky very high up. One stooped to the ground and picked up a hare and went soaring skywards with it, the poor hare squealing all the time. When it was about half-way up to the other eagle it dropped the hare. The higher eagle then stooped at the hare and caught it within ten yards of the ground. They had several rounds like this, and then dropped the hare and went their way - all for sport and devilment."

John Ferguson, Badenoch, tells me that in the course of his long life, on the hill he has at least half a dozen times watched an eagle playing with a branch of juniper or the shin bone of a deer in the air. The eagle would drop the bone then stoop after it, pass it in the air, turn on his back, and catch the bone in one foot. He would sometimes continue to play thus for three-quarters of an hour, and perhaps only three times out of forty would he fail to retrieve the bone (a very hard thing to catch in mid-air). If he did let it drop, he would alight and pick it up from the surface of the snow – there was usually snow on the ground when the eagle played thus.

Ferguson believes the eagle did this to "keep his eye in".

Donald Crerar once watched an eagle playing with a clump of sphagnum moss. The eagle from a height repeatedly dropped the moss, then swooped down and overtook it in the air, and Crerar was positive that the eagle always caught the moss "behind his back" by stretching out one leg behind him to its full extent.

Here is another story from Murdoch Macdonald, central Ross-shire, proving that eagles play or practise the art of catching in mid-air. "I saw two eagles soaring very high. I could see that one of them was carrying something, and when I got my glass on her I saw it was a fairly large clod with heather attached to it, and as it was about the beginning of March I thought she was carrying it for building purposes. She was soaring higher and higher until I could hardly see her, then the clod of earth dropped. When it had fallen some distance the eagle swooped down at lightning speed and caught it again. She again soared to about the same height and let it drop and again caught it, and did the same thing five times in succession. Each time the clod was getting less; there were bits coming off. I often wondered why she did it. Was it practising smartness or playing herself? She certainly didn't want to make any further use of it."

I have mentioned elsewhere that, if one can place credence on the old stories, eagles in former times were much more courageous in defending their eyries than they are nowadays. This change in their habits is only reasonable, because in the days before firearms an eagle could come near a man and give him as good as he received. Nowadays a too daring eagle would in all probability be shot, and so throughout the generations there has been a process of elimination of the most daring members of the race.

Very occasionally, however, an eagle does attack. One stalker writes: "I climbed to the nest and found two young ones in the downy state, and was observing them closely when I heard and felt the swish of wings behind me, the female eagle passing so close to me that I felt the wind from her wings."

James Fraser, west Inverness-shire, writes to me: "I was sitting on the hill with my dog Polly when, to my surprise, I heard an unusual noise above me. Suddenly an old cock grouse dropped between the dog and myself. The dog went in search and found the bird, but instead of retrieving it licked it all over and then allowed the bird to go its own way. I thought no more of this affair. Later in the day I was spying my ground when I was swooped down upon by the same eagle that had dropped the grouse at my feet. The bird caught me by the ankle with its talons, sinking them deep into the flesh, but my dog was soon upon the bird, and with my other foot I managed to kill the eagle, much to my pleasure. Before I could clear the talons from my ankle I had to cut them with my knife. Whether the bird meant to attack me or my dog remains a mystery, but I have a feeling that the dog working with the grouse aroused the anger of the eagle for depriving him of his prey."

I have reports from several sources of an eagle attacking a terrier on the hill by swooping down upon it (see last chapter), and I myself saw a golden eagle upon Beinn MacDhui half swoop at my collie dog Dileas, who was running some distance ahead of me.

M. Matheson, Invergarry, also saw an eagle stoop at a setter. The eagle came down to within twenty yards of the dog then flew right away.

A correspondent writes: "Some years ago I came on an eagle on the flat at the bottom of a narrow gully with steep sides. It was a calm winter day, with six inches of soft snow. I saw that the eagle had seen me, but it made no effort to go, so I went down the slope to see what was wrong with it. When I got to within a couple of yards I stood to see what the eagle was going to do. It had a good look at me, then it walked away towards the slope, up which it went with difficulty on account of the soft snow. When it got up twelve to fifteen yards it turned and looked straight in my face, then spread its wings and flew straight for my face. I happened to have a strong walking-stick, and just as the eagle reached me I jumped to one side and 'let drive' at it as hard as I could, and by a fluke got it on the top of the head. It went down all of a heap in the snow, with wings and tail all over its head. I thought I had killed it, but on looking closely I saw that it was breathing heavily, and by and by up came the head out of the snow, and in a short time the eagle got on its legs, pulled its wings together, and walked across the gully and up the opposite slope a few yards. It had a good look round, then spread its massive wings and flew away down the gully as if nothing had happened, and in a few minutes was soaring in the sky hundreds of feet up.

"Eagles are very fond of rabbits and very destructive to rabbit killers, especially so if they are using snares. I have seen an eagle follow a line of snares at break of day and eat and destroy eight to ten rabbits in a morning."

Sometimes the eagle is caught, for the Duke of Argyll reports the capture of an eagle in a rabbits' snare, but this must be a rare occurrence.

Eagles in Companies   It is seldom that one sees more than two eagles together, except, of course, the family parties in August and September. But occasionally it seems as though eagles do join up into small flocks. On 25th September 1925 no fewer than nine eagles were seen by Duncan Robertson in a west Inverness-shire forest, and F. Mackintosh about the same time saw nine in the neighbouring forest. These were evidently the same birds.

Major Edward Ellice of Invergarry tells me that he has seen eight eagles together, and another correspondent mentions six. It would be interesting to know whether these companies of eagles were young birds of the year migrating. Certainly a pair of eagles will not tolerate a third bird on their "territory," and I have more than once seen such a fierce attack upon an intruder that the feathers flew!

A Fishing Eagle   Mr Robert MacMorran tells me that his father once saw an eagle in the Loch Arkaig district fix on to a salmon in a shallow stream. After much struggling the eagle took the fish on to the bank. The bird had got its talons so deeply embedded in the salmon that it was not able to let go its hold, nor could it lift its booty. Returning the next day, the observer found that the eagle had escaped. The fish lay with its back torn where the eagle's talons had been drawn out, otherwise it was untouched.

Loch Arkaig was one of the last haunts of the osprey in Scotland, and this incident would seem to refer to the osprey rather than to the eagle, but the observer, living in the district and being interested in birds, was not likely to mistake osprey for eagle.

The Eagle's love for the High Tops   There is nothing that gives the golden eagle more pleasure than to perch upon the topmost pinnacle of some rock, or upon the cairn that marks the summit of some high hill, there to bask in the rays of the summer sun and look sternly upon each surrounding hill, glen, and corrie.

On The last Sunday of May 1926 I happened to climb to the south-west top of Brae Riach. The ground here is over 4100 feet above sea-level, and although it was so late in the season there had been a heavy fall of snow which covered the ground to the depth of two feet. As I had climbed I had noticed a golden eagle soaring high above me, and on the hill-top I saw in the soft snow a perfect impression of the great primary wing-feathers. The bird had evidently been amusing itself by walking about in the soft snow with its wings outspread. There was not a single track of bird or animal in the snow beside its own, so that it cannot have been in pursuit of any quarry.

The sun shone brilliantly that day, and the snow was so dazzling that I had walked only a little way across the plateau when I felt snow blindness coming on.

Dogs suffer readily from snow blindness; it would be interesting to know whether the eagle is immune.

W. J. Shaw, Inverness, writes as follows: "In the year 1890 my father, then tenant of the farm of Oldtoun, Stratherrick, had what I consider a unique experience. One day in April he was having a round of the sheep, and on the plateau just north of the Pass of Inverfarigaig he heard what he thought were the cries of a child in distress. Crossing a small knoll he saw two golden eagles in deadly embrace. As he approached them he thought the undermost bird caught sight of him, but it was held down by its antagonist, which was so absorbed in the struggle that it paid no heed to his approach. He caught the top bird by the wings and placed his foot on the under one. Searching his pockets, he found he had nothing to tie the wings with, ultimately doing so with a bandage removed from an injured hand. Meantime the other bird had by degrees pulled itself free, and after several attempts managed to soar away. At a cottar's house a sack was procured, and, unaware of the risk he ran, my father carried the monarch of the air home on his back.

"Both were male birds, the captured one, a very fine specimen, measuring 7 feet from tip to tip of its wings. The capture was kept in an attic room for six weeks, being fed on hares, rabbits, and dead lambs. He rarely touched the food in our presence, but we enjoyed viewing operations through the keyhole.

Fights between Golden Eagles

THE COCK EAGLE ARRIVES WITH A GROUSE HELD IN ONE FOOT. SWARMS OF
FLIES CAN BE SEEN RISING FROM THREE CARCASES. CAIN GREETS HER
FATHER WITH A BOW, WHILE ABEL IS LYING PANTING ON THE LOWER EDGE OF
THE EYRIE ON THE RIGHT OF THE PICTURE.

"Through the agency of the late Mr. Thomas Henderson of the Highland Club the bird was sent to the Zoological Gardens, London, where it was an object of considerable interest because of its unique capture.

"An incident difficult to explain occurred about a week after the eagle was captured. The attic window, a small one about 2 feet by 1½ feet, opened on hinges and was protected by wire netting. On the occasion referred to the bird had the window partly opened, and was just on the verge of escape when discovered. To our astonishment we were informed from two different, both absolutely reliable, sources that on that day and hour two eagles were seen soaring over the house. How did they discover the place of imprisonment? Had they any means of communication? It could scarcely be a coincidence, as never before or after was an eagle seen in the vicinity of the farmhouse."

A fight to the death between two golden eagles must be a magnificent sight and one that is very rarely seen. John MacDonald, a head stalker in Inverness-shire, writes: "I did not see the fight myself, but my youngest boy did. I came on the scene immediately afterwards and picked up the dead eagle, the other fluttering off amongst the trees. It was scarcely able to rise off the ground, but we failed to capture it. The dead eagle's gullet was torn completely out of the throat. They were both male birds, and I expect the fight originated over a hen eagle, as it happened during the mating season.

Another stalker, Duncan MacRae, witnessed a fight between two eagles which ended indecisively. "It was in spring-time," he says, "and the two eagles were about two hundred yards up when they 'clinched' and came down 'heads and tails.' I looked out for a bad smash, but when about twenty feet from the ground they let go. They stood on the ground for some time facing each other, staring at one another with necks out and feathers ruffled. Then they rose and each flew away in opposite directions."

CHAPTER 20

THE COUNTRY OF THE EAGLE

<small>LOCH A'AN OF THE HIGH CAIRNGORMS: MIDSUMMER</small>

There are two unusually grand lochs in the Highlands of Scotland where the golden eagle has his home – Loch A'an and Loch Coruisk.

Loch A'an is in the Central Highlands; Loch Coruisk is in the Isle of Skye, only a few hundred yards from the Atlantic. Loch Coruisk (or, as it should correctly be spelled, Loch Coruisge) lies beneath the Black Cuillin; Loch A'an is in the very heart of the Cairngorms.

Loch A'an is in Gaelic Loch Ath-fhinn, the *th* and the *ft* being mute. The derivation of the word is doubtful, but it is believed to mean the ford of Fionn or Fingal, the legendary hero of the Gaels.

Although the hills rise high above it, Loch A'an itself lies higher than many a hilltop. Its clear waters are 2400 feet above the sea, and it is May before it is released from the grip of the ice. The hills guard it well. Northward Cairngorm (4084 feet) rises sheer; to the south are the steep, rocky slopes of Beinn Mheadhon (the Middle Hill). West is the great bulk of Beinn MacDhui (MacDuff's Hill). And so Loch A'an is invisible from the low ground, and is difficult to see even from the Cairngorms themselves. But there is one place from which Loch A'an is seen in all its grandeur, and that is the head of the magnificent alpine corrie which rises to Beinn MacDhui from the western shore of the loch.

One brilliant July morning of great heat a companion and I left Rothiemurchus Forest in the Spey valley and climbed to the great tableland which extends from Cairngorm to Beinn MacDhui. In the forest the heat was drawing from the old pines a rich scent; amongst the heather below the trees the blaeberries were almost ripe and the heather buds already showed their colour. Before we had reached the high tops clouds hid the sun, and a warm southerly wind brought refreshing rain. How green were the high plateaux and corries of the Cairngorms that July day! The heat had been exceptional, and periodic thundershowers had refreshed the ground.

Red deer are quick to climb to the hill-tops when there is pasture for them thus high, and to-day beside Lochan Buidhe, the highest tarn in all Scotland, a herd of about a hundred and fifty hinds were feeding. Lochan Buidhe is not far short of 4000 feet above the sea. It is a shallow, very clear tarn, almost at the watershed between Dee and Spey. Its waters flow to the A'an, thence to the Spey; a hundred yards from it is a small stream which joins the Dee in the pass below the lochan.

Many of the hinds which were grazing on the fresh green grass beside Lochan Buidhe had their month-old calves with them, and one heard the soft, high-pitched bleating of the calves and the deeper calls of the mothers as they answered. Across a carpet of countless green alpine plants we walked, and soon reached the edge of the tableland and looked down upon dark Loch A'an, encircled by stupendous black cliffs. How often the golden eagle passes across this plateau at his hunting! I have seen him sailing backwards and forwards in play through a host of fleeing ptarmigan, yet never attempting to strike down one of the terrified birds. I have seen him greet the rising sun from the hill-top, perched upon some rocky pinnacle, and at evening I have seen him on broad dark wings sail in to the ledge where he would pass the long winter night.

We were now at the head of a wild corrie with a swift flowing stream. Below us was a great snowfield of immense depth. Despite the heat the snow was hard and icy. At its margin the grass was brown; a few yards away it was green and in vigorous growth after its long imprisonment. Beside the snow, a wheatear perched, and a pair of meadow pipits rose near it. As we stood there, looking down upon the loch, a heavy thundershower quickly formed. It screened Loch A'an but passed us by, and with its passing the blue sky once more appeared, and great thunder-clouds, on which the evening sun shone golden, floated in the upper air.

We descended into the corrie. The snows were melting so quickly that the burn had risen to a torrent of clear, foaming waters; we followed these waters to the edge of the cliff and saw them leap to Loch A'an in a series of splendid waterfalls.

Three impetuous streams meet in the corrie, and in the still, warm air was a deep, continuous surge, as of the waves of the ocean breaking upon some distant shore.

In the corrie were many alpine plants. Deep blue violets (they are three months later in flowering here than in the glens below) were drenched with the spray of the waterfalls, and the paler blue flowers of the butterwort (*pinguicula*) were growing from damp niches of the rocks. Here, too, the white petals of the starry saxifrage (each with the small characteristic yellow mark at the base) were showing, and the yellow blooms of the globe flower (*trollius*). Lower down, near the base of the corrie, delicate harebells were opening their blue flowers, and at 2700 feet I passed a raspberry bush – I have never before seen one thus high.

Twilight was falling as we reached the foot of the corrie. A soft, kindly light bathed the snowfields and the young green plants that grew so near them. Over the rocks at the head of the corrie the waters of the Feith Bhuidhe (the Yellow Stream) flowed invisible beneath a great snowfield, the remains of a storm that had swept over the hills from the west at the New Year. From beneath a wide arch of snow the waters emerged, hurrying downwards in a foaming tumult to where Loch A'an, mother-like, awaited their coming and quietened their youthful brawling.

South of Loch A'an a great precipice rises. In a past age huge fragments of rock have been hurled from its summit and now lie in confusion beside the loch. One of the largest of these boulders is balanced upon other lesser rocks in such a way that a recess is formed below it, capable of sheltering and concealing many persons. This is Clach Dion, or, in English, the Shelter Stone, which for centuries has been used as a sleeping-place by hunters, and more recently by climbers and mountain lovers. Beside the Shelter Stone this July night the air was warm and still, and was perfumed by the young crowberry shoots. The alpine vegetation here is unusually luxuriant. The blaeberry plants are taller even than in the forest, but whereas in the forest the fruits had already become deep blue and ripe, here, at 2500 feet above the sea, they were as yet small and green. Growing amongst the common blaeberry (or bilberry as it is sometimes called) one saw plants of the great bilberry, distinguished by their glaucous leaves and more woody stems. The great bilberry rarely fruits in the Cairngorms, and now for the first time (perhaps because of the warm summer) I saw blossoms, and here and there berries commencing to form. In one place there was a carpet of cloudberries, with many fruits already large and red upon them. It is curious that the fruit of the cloudberry should be red when imperfectly ripe and when mature should change to yellow.

A few hundred yards below us Loch A'an lay, with calm, opal-tinted waters. Many trout were "rising" on the loch and were breaking the mirror-like surface. It was now two hours from midnight. We walked to the shore of the loch and seated ourselves beside a sandy bay where the united hill streams enter the loch. The water was extraordinarily clear. Even at that hour of the night we could see the trout cruising near the surface – dark, tenuous figures against the light pebbles on the bed of the loch. We could follow the course of an individual fish, and watch it rise to the surface every few seconds and suck down some small fly or midge. Once a black trout encroached on its neighbour's "beat" and was immediately driven off by the rightful occupier – a trout of much lighter colour.

At half-past ten, when the twilight was deepening, a goosander flew silently up the loch on white wings and alighted with a splash in very shallow water beside the estuary of the stream. She – it was a goosander duck – had not observed us, and after preening her feathers commenced to fish carefully. Stealthily she swam around, craning her neck forward at each stroke of her feet, and some of the trout on seeing her hurried out into deep water. Once she made a sudden rush, but it was too dark to see whether she caught her fish. I do not think she can have been really hungry, because when she was comparatively near us, and in shallow water, a trout swam unsuspectingly past her and we made sure she would capture it. But her pursuit was faint-hearted and the trout easily escaped her. After this she took wing, and on ghostly, silent wings disappeared down the loch in the dusk.

Beside the Shelter Stone was the small "earth" of a fox, and an old cock grouse, disturbed in his slumbers, rose at our feet as we made our way back to the stone, and called loudly and cheerily.

We had decided to spend the short summer night below the Shelter Stone, but the recess seemed dark and depressing on so warm and still a night, and so we made our couch on a narrow, heather-strewn shelf out in the open, but protected from dew or rain by an overhanging corner of the great boulder towering above. On this shelf we lay and dozed, with the noise of falling water in our ears and the peace and silence of the hills around us.

At midnight the sky was clear, and a single star burned in the depth of Loch A'an. An hour later thin mists began to form on the slopes of Beinn Mheadhon. They grew steadily though imperceptibly, and at sunrise a dense billowy cloud lay upon the loch. That cloud crept toward us, as surely and inexorably as the rising tide, and an hour after sunrise we were enveloped in grey, motionless vapours that seemed to deaden the murmur of the waterfalls above us. But even in the damp mist at dawn the air was oppressively warm, and so we waited unchilled upon our hard couch in the hopes that the mist would lift with the strengthening of the sun.

We were not disappointed. Shortly after eleven o'clock the sharp summit of the great cliff known as the Sticil, which rises almost sheer from the Shelter Stone, loomed ghostly through the thinning cloud, and at length the whole precipice, dark and grim even on a fine summer morning, stood revealed.

A narrow gully in that cliff was snow-filled; high up on the face of the precipice we noticed a curious hollow, large and circular. It seemed as though a stream may at certain times issue from here; there is a resemblance in it to Ossian's cave in Glencoe, but, unlike that cave, it appears to be inaccessible. It is not so long ago that a pair of golden eagles had their eyrie in the face of the Sticil, but I do not think they build there now, although their eyrie was safe from even the most daring climber.

Before midday the mist was rising everywhere. In soft woolly balls the clouds hung on the sides of the great snowy corrie of the Geur Uisge, then gradually dissolved. As we left Clach Dion a pair of meadow pipits were courting beside the stone and the sun was striving to pierce the upper clouds. The burn had fallen considerably – for at night, even though the weather remains warm, the melting of the snow is slower than during the day – and whereas the evening before we crossed it with difficulty, it now presented no obstacle. Near the snow the blaeberry plants were not yet in flower, although in the forest below their fruit was already ripe, and the alpine ferns had only just commenced to unroll their fronds. Everywhere violets were in blossom, and at one place a cushion of *Draba rupestris* grew among the rocks. As we had climbed the corrie to the snows near its crest the mists had collected into a compact grey cloud above Loch A'an, and now, rising into the corrie itself, they pressed upward towards us, and soon we were walking through a grey, impenetrable cloud. We continued our climb, with the stream as our guide, until we knew that our course lay north - towards the Spey valley. Soon a grey wall of snow rose up straight in our path. It towered almost vertically above us, its top invisible in cloud. Along the base of this mysterious phantom-like wall we groped our way, and all the time we could hear the calling of many hinds and their calves, hidden somewhere in the close mist. By compass and aneroid we kept our course, and just as we reached the hill-top at 4000 feet we climbed out of the mist and saw the summits of many hills rising from the vast cloud that covered all the lower grounds. The valley of the Dee was invisible, and the Spey, although so near to us, was unseen. We looked deep into the Lairig Ghru and saw that this hill-pass, too, was enveloped in a white, motionless cloud. Above this mist-sea a swift darted and wheeled in the warm still air, and from a dark cloud high above us came the mutter of thunder.

As we descended to the Lairig we once again entered the clouds,

THE AUTHOR ON THE 'HIGH TOPS'.

and found in the pass twilight gloom and chilly air, so that we thought with envy of the wheeling swift, and the hinds and their calves enjoying the warmth and clear air of the high tops of the Cairngorms.

CHAPTER 21

TRADITIONS OF THE EAGLE

"The eagle suffers little birds to sing." – Shakespeare, *Titus Andronicus*

There are more myths woven around the eagle than any other bird. This is due, I think, not so much to its appearance or to its habits or size, as to the power of its wings.

No one who has watched the eagle can doubt that it rises into the blue vault of the sky from the pure joy of flight, and since the eagle soars upward in happiness, it has inspired human beings with uplifting thoughts throughout the ages, for has not man always sought inspiration from above?

It is probable that most, if not all, of the myths and legends of the eagle originated in the East, whence so many of the Celtic beliefs have their origin. In the Rig-Veda the sun is compared to an eagle hovering in the air, and the eagle is connected with many other Oriental solar myths.

152

The eagle was the standard of the Assyrians, of the Persians, and of the Romans. Representations of eagles were used upon Babylonian sceptres. On the sceptre of Zeus was an eagle, and on the altar at Olympia there was an eagle with outstretched wings.

One of the Assyrian deities, Nisroch by name, was eagle-headed, and perhaps because of this the Persians adopted the eagle as their standard and the Persian kings had an eagle on their sceptre. The Persians reverenced the eagle, and admired the aquiline nose, which they tried to cultivate in themselves.

The Greek mythology of the eagle is so complicated that the great scholar, Professor D'Arcy Thomson, is of opinion that it baffles analysis. Many of us have read how Hebe, the Goddess of Youth, was cup-bearer to Jupiter, but lost her post because she tripped and fell on a solemn occasion. Jupiter accordingly had to go in quest of another cup-bearer, and, to facilitate his search, assumed the form of an eagle. He had not flown far when he beheld a youth of marvellous beauty alone on a hill. He swooped down, caught him in his mighty talons, and bore him off to Olympus. The youth whom Jupiter had taken for the duties of cup-bearer to the gods was Ganymede, son of the King of Troy. This incident is supposed to refer in some hidden way to the constellation Aquila; it appears on some Greek coins.

The beautiful Leda, who took the form of a swan, was once, Euripides tells, pursued by an eagle. Fights between eagle and swan often occur in Greek literature and appear on coins. The eagle is also associated with the dolphin. This is sometimes considered to be symbolic of the fish trade, and sometimes believed to have an astronomical meaning.

The Etruscans were supposed to understand the language of eagles.

There is an Egyptian legend that the eagle lays three eggs, and after careful choice retains one and breaks the other two. According to that old legend, the reason for this curious behaviour is that the eagle sheds its talon at this season and so cannot rear three young.

Aristotle, Pliny, and others said that the eagle lays three eggs, hatches two, but rears only one eaglet, and so it seems that in those days, as now, one of the eaglets was in the habit of killing the other.

The Greeks believed that the eagle went without food while brooding.

ABEL, LEFT ALONE, SPENDS HIS TIME DOING WING EXERCISES.

Pliny and others mention that the gall of the eagle mixed with honey makes an ointment for the eyes. They say also that the eagle forces its young to look straight at the sun, and that "the bastards, by this test being discovered, are cast out." Chaucer quotes this old legend, which is apparently of Egyptian origin.

It was believed that the eagle was exempt from thirst but perished from hunger; that its right wing, buried in the ground, was an insurance against hail; that it walked with its toes turned in to keep its claws sharp.

An eagle is said to have brought Venus' slipper to Mercury. Professor D'Arcy Thomson believes that the eagle sometimes stands for a stellar emblem and sometimes for a solar one. In its battles with the hare, swan, bull, dragon, and so forth, these latter are probably symbolic of their stellar namesakes, and here the eagle is doubtless a stellar emblem and not a solar one.

Æsop, who lived some six hundred years before Christ, has some charming fables of the eagle.

"There was once," says Æsop, "a hare being pursued by an eagle. The hare betook himself to the nest of the beetle, whom he entreated to save him. The beetle therefore interceded with the eagle, begging of him not to kill the poor suppliant, and conjuring him, by mighty Jupiter, not to slight his intercession and break the laws of hospitality because he was so small an animal. But the eagle, in wrath, gave the beetle a flap with his wing and straightway seized upon the hare and devoured him. When the eagle flew away the beetle flew after him, to learn where his nest was, and getting into it rolled out the eagle's eggs one by one and broke them. The eagle, grieved and enraged to think that anyone should attempt so audacious a thing, built his nest next time in a higher place; but the beetle got at it again and served him in the same manner as before. Upon this the eagle, being at a loss what to do, flew up to Jupiter, his lord and king, and placed the third brood of eggs as a sacred deposit in his lap, begging him to guard them for him. But the beetle, having made a little ball of dirt, flew up with it and dropped it in Jupiter's lap. The King of the Gods rose up suddenly to shake off the dirt, and, forgetting the eggs, threw them down and they were again broken. The beetle boldly told Jupiter that he had done this to be revenged upon the eagle, who had not only wronged him but had acted impiously towards Jove himself. So when the eagle came in Jupiter told him that the beetle was the aggrieved party and that he had complained not without reason. But Jupiter, being unwilling that the race of eagles should be diminished, advised the beetle to come to an accommodation with the eagle. The plucky beetle would not agree to this, and so Jupiter transferred the eagle's breeding to another season when there are no beetles to be seen."

Another of Æsop's fables concerns an eagle and a jackdaw. "An eagle made a sweep from a high rock and carried off a lamb. A jackdaw who saw the thing happen, thinking he could do likewise, bore down with all the force he could muster upon a ram, intending to bear him off as a prize. But his claws became entangled in the wool, and he made such a fluttering in his efforts to escape that the shepherd, seeing through the whole matter, came up and caught him, and having clipped his wings, carried him home to his children at nightfall. 'What bird is this that you have brought us, father?' exclaimed the children. 'Why,' said he, 'if you ask him he will tell you he is an eagle, but if you will take my word for it I know him to be but a jackdaw."

Aristotle in his *Historia Animalium* mentions that the eagle is said to become weary of caring for the young and extrudes one from the nest. The lammergeier is said to feed the eaglet after its parents have turned it out. "The eagle abstains from food to avoid harrying the young of other animals; that is to say, its wings blanch, and for some days its talons get turned awry." In its old age the upper mandible grows longer and more crooked, and the bird eventually dies of starvation. "Thus is the eagle punished, for it was once a man, and in human form refused entertainment to a stranger." That is an Egyptian myth taken by Aristotle.

In Celtic poetry there are many references to the eagle.

In "Cumha an Fhir Mhoir" in *Dan an Deirg* we read:

> "Bha t'airde mar dharach 'sa' ghleann,
>   Do luaths, mar *iolair* nam beann, gun gheilt."
> "Your height was as an oak in the glen,
>   Your speed as an eagle of the mountains, without fear."

In "Tiomna Ghuill" we read:

> "Luath mar *fhireun* an athair,
>   's an ioma-ghaoth na platha fo sgiathaibh."

> "Swift as an eagle of the air,
>   And the whirlwind as a flash under its wings."

And

> "Mar *iolair* leont air carraig nan cnoc,
> 'Sa sgiath air a lot le dealan na h-oidche."
> "As a wounded eagle on the rock of the knolls,
>   And its wing wounded by the lightning of the night."

The primary feathers of the eagle – "ite dhosrach an fhirein," "the bushy feather of the eagle " – have from earliest times been worn as a mark of rank.

A Highland chief wears in his bonnet three eagle's feathers, a chieftain two, and a gentleman one eagle's feather.

Eagles' feathers were used as arrows, and the best arrows were fashioned from the feathers of the eagles of Loch Treig in Lochaber. There is an old quatrain

> "Bogha dh'uibhar Easragain,
>   Ite firein Locha Treig,
>   Ceir bhuidhe Bhaile na Gailbhinn,
>   'S ceann bho'n cheard MacPheadrain."

> "The yew-bow of Easragain,
>   The eagle's feather from Loch Treig,
>   The yellow wax from Baile na Gailbbinn,
>   And the head from the smith MacPheadrain."

No Highlander was considered a finished sportsman until he had shot with his bow and arrow the three monarchs – the eagle of the air, the "royal" stag of the earth, the wild swan of the water.

Eagles' feathers must have been used in many countries for arrows. Æschylus, who lived five hundred years before the birth of Christ, writes (*Fragment* 123, Plumtre's translation):

> "So in the Libyan fable it is told
> That once an eagle, stricken with a dart,
> Said, when he saw the fashion of the shaft
> 'With our own feathers, not by others' hands
> Are we now smitten.'

Byron (*English Bards and Scotch Reviewers*, line 826) writes:

> "So the struck eagle, stretched upon the plain,
> No more through rolling clouds to soar again,

> Viewed his own feather on the fatal dart,
>
> And wing'd the shaft that quivered in his heart."

Edmund Waller. (1605–87), in his ode "To a Lady Singing a Song of his Composing," writes:

> "The eagle's fate and mine are one,
>
> Which on the shaft that made him die,
>
> Espied a feather of his own,
>
> Wherewith he wont to soar so high."

There is a curious Bulgarian legend of St George in which the eagle is mentioned. The saint had been thrown by his brothers into a deep well. He who in the depths of that well met the black ram was borne to the realms of darkness; he who met the white ram was carried forthwith to the realms of light. St George encounters the black ram and is therefore taken to the realm of darkness. While there he meets a fierce dragon who is menacing the king's daughter. He kills the dragon and rescues the maiden. Scarcely has he done this when he sees a huge poisonous snake. The snake is climbing a tree, high up in which is an eagle's eyrie, with eaglets in it. In the nick of time St George kills the snake, and the eagle in gratitude bears him on his wings from dark to light.

The eagle is generally known as the King of Birds, but the following narrative seems to show that in olden times it was believed that one particular bird ruled as king over all the birds of the world. The story is given in the *Transactions of the Gaelic Society of Inverness*, under date about forty years ago, and was taken down from an old Athole "seannachaidh" (tale-teller) many years before that.

"For ages before the foundations of the old Black Castle of Moulin were laid (and its history lies before all written record), famous falcons under the king's special protection built their nests undisturbed in the rock above Moulin every season, till once upon a time, just as the falcon was preparing to lay, a huge old raven came from Badenoch, from the haunted Forest of Gaick, and by its superior strength drove the poor falcon away from its newly finished nest.

"However, there seems to have been more justice going on amongst the fowls of the air than amongst men, for after the falcon had used every possible means to dislodge the raven without success, it at last rose in wheeling circles higher and higher, till it was almost out of sight, then flew straight away southwards and the good men of Athole thought they had seen the last of their famous hawks. Such, however, was not to be, for on the seventh day the falcon reappeared, coming from the south, accompanied by a 'smart, slim, long-winged white bird' (eun caol, sgairteil, gadsgaithach, geal), making straight for the nest. As soon as the old raven saw them coming it rose in a great flurry off the nest and flew to meet them, croaking out an apology to the stranger for its misbehaviour to the falcon. This apology, however, seemed of no avail, as the stranger with one stroke of its wing dashed out the raven's brains, at the same time losing a feather from his own wing. Then he flew round for a little time until he saw the falcon once more take possession of her hereditary nest, and then rose above the clouds and flew southwards, and was never seen in Athole since." The lost feather was picked up, and was found to be so hard that, as the "seannachaidh" put it – "that feather was so hard it would cut a shaving of the hardest oak plank in the Howe of Moulin," and he used always to conclude the story by saying very earnestly, "Agus 's e Righ nan Eun a bh'ann" ("And that was the King of Birds").

There is an old tale in the Outer Hebrides that there was once a king of Erin who lost the sight of his eyes and the strength of his feet, and his youngest son set out for the Green Isle – the enchanted island beyond the western main where dwells eternal youth – for the magic water that would heal his father. On his wanderings he met a giant, and the giant told him that an eagle would bear him on its wings to the Green Isle, if only he could cut off the wart on the eagle with his sword without drawing a drop of blood. The king's son did this, and the eagle said to him, "Now come on the root of my two wings, for I know thy matter better than thou dost thyself." And the eagle bore him away and away until they reached the Green Isle, and there he was able to fill his bottle with the magic water of healing.

The following tale is still told in Lochaber. Many years ago winter tarried in the Highlands until long after her accustomed season. Beltane (the first day of May) dawned with a frost so intense that the old eagle who had his eyrie on the cliffs above

Loch Treig felt the icy air even through his thick plumage that had withstood the most severe storm of the winter. Although he was of a great age – is there not a Gaelic proverb, "As old as the Loch Treig eagle"? – he knew that a water-ousel that lived where the river left the loch was older even than he. Accordingly he spread his wings and sailed down the loch to inquire from the water-ousel whether, in all its long life, it had ever known so cold a Beltane dawn. The eagle found the water-ousel searching for food in the icy bed of the stream. When it saw the eagle it flew up, and first sang him a cheery song, partly to keep itself warm, partly as a welcome to the King of Birds. "Tell me," said the eagle, "have you in all your long years of living ever felt so cold a Beltane dawn?" "No," said the water-ousel, "but there is an old blackbird down in the thicket yonder who is older than I. He may be able to tell you of an even colder Beltane." The eagle flew off. He soon heard the flute-like notes of the blackbird from the leafless bushes and swooped down. "Good morning to you, blackbird," said he; "have you ever felt the like of this at Beltane before? It makes even the sun-fire in my blood run cold." "Well, no," said the blackbird, "I have never, indeed, seen the like, but there is a stag in yonder corrie older even than I. He may have seen a colder Beltane." So the eagle soared up to the corrie where the snow was lying as deep as at midwinter. He saw the old stag, very thin and dejected, scraping away the snow with his forefeet as he searched for the brown grass, with scarcely any nourishment in it, that was buried below the snow. So busy was the stag he did not hear the rush of the eagle's wings, and was astonished when the eagle called out to him, " Good morning to you, O stag; is not this the cold Beltane? Did you ever see the like in all your time?" "Well," said the stag, "I never saw the like, but down in the loch yonder is an old trout. He is the oldest of all living things in Lochaber, and it is possible he may be able to remember a colder Beltane." Again the eagle took wing. He sailed down to the dark waters and called to the trout. But it was long before the trout heard him, because he was in the very deepest part of the loch trying to find some warmth from the bitter cold, and, of course, the deepest water was the warmest.

The old trout shivered as he came to the surface, but he was always most courteous, and gave good-day to the eagle. The King of Birds repeated his question and this time he received a different answer. "Yes," said the old trout, "many, many years ago, perhaps before you were even an egg, I remember a Beltane day that was colder even than this. On that day I, being young, leaped from the loch with my body in an arch and, would you believe it, I was frozen stiff and rigid before ever I touched the water again." "Ah," said the eagle, "that must in truth have been the great cold." And, at last satisfied, he sailed back to his eyrie and, we may suppose, comforted his mate as she brooded her two eggs.

CHAPTER 22

THE COUNTRY OF THE EAGLE

<small>AUTUMN IN THE ISLE OF SKYE</small>

"Who satisfieth thy mouth with good things; so that thy youth is renewed like the
eagle's." – Psalm ciii 5.

In the dawn, still and grey, Loch Slapin seemed to sleep.
Northward the rocky flanks of Blaven towered to meet grey
clouds, drifted slowly on the dun wind of western seas.

Across the ocean leagues the hills of Mull rose; on the distant
southern horizon they towered above the lesser heights of
Ardnamurchan – Beinn Mhor, of rounded and symmetrical
summit, Beinn Tailaidh, and Duin da Ghaoithe (the Hill of the
Two Winds).

At full daylight we sailed westward from Loch Slapin, and as
we passed the Spar Cave and rounded Rudha na h'Easgainne we
met the long Atlantic swell that swept shoreward from afar.

Soon we were in sight of Loch Scavaig, and as we sailed toward the lonely loch we looked upon what must surely be the most magnificent view in all Scotland.

The loch bites far into the land and it divides near the shore. Here are Cammasiunary of the pale sands and, a few miles west, the deep basin in which Loch Coruisk lies.

From Loch Scavaig the magnificent range of the Black Cuillin towers to the skies. The peaks rise in rocky spires, in jagged walls of black cliff, in grim buttresses. About these aerial spires the golden eagle soars, and in the old days had the sea eagle or erne as his companion. But now the erne has gone and the golden eagle – iolaire dubh, he is called in the Gaelic – has the Cuillin to himself. A stalker told me that when climbing Blaven one winter he had found a golden eagle lying dead on that hill. The bird bore the marks of a desperate fight, and when, a few days later, the stalker read in the local paper of a fight between an eagle and a wild cat in Ross-shire, he felt convinced that the eagle he had found had drifted south after the battle to die on the Cuillin of Skye.

At all times there is mystery in the Cuillin, and on a grey day of autumn as that of which I write the mystery is intensified.

The hills seem to hold deep secrets; to live in other and incredibly distant times, the time of that traditional hunt among the hills when six thousand deer were slain by three thousand hounds. The Cuillin are unique among Scottish mountains. They seem to belong to a world apart, and have affinity with the needle-like peaks of distant Spitsbergen rather than with the hills of the Scottish mainland.

Although the skies were grey when we sailed into Loch Scavaig the air was very clear, and, peak upon peak, the Cuillin stood out deep blue and wrapped about with the mysterious hill silence

We sailed into Loch na Cuilce (the inner basin of Loch Scavaig) and dropped anchor beneath Allt a' Chaoich, the Mad Burn, which dashes to the sea in a series of foaming cascades. Scott, in the *Lord of the Isles*, writes thus of that burn:

"Where a wild stream, with headlong shock,
Came brawling down its bed of rock
To mingle with the main."

The tide was low when we landed where the burn which flows

from Loch Coruisk enters the sea, and in a minute had climbed the small ridge and looked on to the waters of Loch Coruisk. That loch lies less than two hundred yards from the sea. Its waters are dark always; to-day they were mirror-like, and here and there the inky surface was disturbed by a rising sea-trout. In summer a colony of light-winged sea swallows have their home on an island on Loch Coruisk, but in autumn they are fishing in the sunlit seas of the Equator, and there is then a great silence above the loch.

Immediately east of the loch Sgurr na Stri, the Peak of the Conflict, rises; west, Garsven towers to a height of just on 3000 feet. Its precipitous slopes are almost covered with boulders and scree, but here and there are little "pockets" of green grass and alpine plants. On one such green "oasis" among the stones three stags were spied feeding, and up the steep hill we forthwith commenced to climb, the stalker (carrying the rifle) setting the pace, I following him, and the young sportsman who hoped that day to account for his first stag bringing up the rear.

We climbed along the course of a clear burn, with pale green pools and white shallows. The heather bloom was withered, yet its scent still hung in the air. At 2000 feet the blue scabious showed its deep-tinted flowers; the starry saxifrage was over, but amongst the scree the fronds of the parsley fern were still green.

An hour after midday shafts of blue appeared in the grey sky, and upon the three slender spires of Sgurr nan Gillean the sunlight burned awhile. Backward and forward across the black precipices of Sgurr Dubh a golden eagle soared, with the joy of skilled flight, indifferent to the immense abyss beneath him.

Two thousand feet below us Loch Coruisk lay, a dark loch cradled in a dark corrie. Loch Scavaig was dark too, except beside its farther shore where its waters, lying above sand, seemed diffused with a wonderful emerald glow.

We had now reached a corrie above that in which the stags were grazing, but separated from it by a steep ridge which hid us from the deer. The stalker and the sportsman accordingly crossed the ridge and I continued the climb alone.

Steeper and ever steeper became the ascent, and at last I came upon a narrow knife-like ridge, and looked into the corrie southward over a sheer cliff several hundred feet in height. A hind was feeding on a small grassy strip of ground surrounded by a wilderness of scree, but from where I stood I could see no sign of the stags, and, lest I should disturb the stalk, I retraced my steps a few yards and continued my climb on the far side of the ridge.

From the north a golden eagle approached. Close above my head he sailed, so that I could see each splendid primary wing-feather with the sky showing between them. His golden head was lowered as he carefully scanned the ground beneath him, and he barely heeded me as he passed. He disappeared into the corrie where were the stalkers and the stags, but almost at once returned, then once more entered the corrie, flying even lower than before.

From near the top of Garsven I looked across Loch Coruisk to where the moist black walls of Blaven glistened.

Across Loch Slapin, beyond Dunscaith and Sleat, many hills rose – the peaks of Knoydart, Ben Screel, and, farther north, the shapely Sisters of Kintail. Upon the heights of the Island of Rhum – they, too, are known as the Cuillin – sun and shade alternated. Eigg was in shadow, but on Canna was sunshine.

Rhum, Canna, Eigg, and Muck form what is known as the parish of the Small Isles. From Eigg have come beautiful old Gaelic airs and sacred runes, and until recently the island was the home of one who has done much to keep alive the songs and traditions of the Gael.

Faintly across the spires of the Black Cuillin of Skye the hills of Harris rose. There was sun upon those distant hills, but above the peaks around me the sky momentarily was darkening and the hill silence seemed to become intensified.

From beyond Sgurr Dearg a raven sailed swiftly and eagerly southward. In a couple of minutes his mate followed him, croaking as she passed, so that her hoarse cries echoed in the corrie.

Bird-life is scarce on the Cuillin. I saw no single ptarmigan, and, the country of the grouse was far below me. In autumn wild geese sometimes cross these hills on their southward migration. One September morning a gaggle of geese passed, calling in alarm. Above them a peregrine falcon circled, then stooped at terrific speed upon a goose, bearing it, still alive, to the ground. The remaining geese regathered themselves into their accustomed formation and sped southward. The peregrine was disturbed at his "kill," and the goose taken from him by a sportsman who had witnessed the occurrence. No goose, I understand, ever tasted better. (In Chapter 18 I have given a story of an eagle attacking a goose.)

At evening a grey shower drifted over Marsco, then the clouds dispersed, and Loch Scavaig and its sentinel peaks were bathed in the soft sunshine of the west. At sunset the western sky was afire, and after dusk the full moon, low on the horizon, shone upon the soft clouds that rested lightly on Blaven of the black cliffs.

That evening I saw the stalkers, and learned from them that they had accounted for their stag in that high-lying corrie of Garsven, and with great difficulty had dragged the animal to the sea over 2000 feet below them. But long before evening I had known of their success, for the hurried flight of the ravens into the corrie and their eager croaks told me that one of the stags of the Black Cuillin had met his fate.

CHAPTER 23

THE STATUS OF THE GOLDEN AND SEA EAGLES,
PAST AND PRESENT

"Full oft the eagle screamed, dewy of wings."

The line which heads this chapter was probably the first record of the eagle in British literature. It is found in an Anglo-Saxon Chronicle, called *Codex Exoniensis*, of date about A.D. 580, and occurs in a poem called "The Perils of the Seafarer."

In 1526 Boece wrote in his *Cosmographe and Description of Albion:* "Of fowles such as live by plunder there are sundry kinds in Scotland; as eagles…"

In 1577 a writer called John Harrison wrote a book on *Hawkes and Rauenous Fowles*. In it he describes golden eagles nesting at Castle Dinas Bran in Denbyshire.

167

In 1776 to 1786 seventy eagles were killed in five parishes of Deeside, according to Sim's *Vertebrate Fauna of Dee*.

In 1797 Bewick, the great naturalist of the north of England, describes four species of eagles in Britain, namely, the ring-tailed eagle, the golden eagle, the sea eagle, and the white-tailed or cinereous eagle. Later it was realised that this was an error, and that there were really only two species, namely, the golden eagle and the white-tailed or sea eagle. Bewick had named the immature form of the golden eagle the ring-tailed eagle, and the immature form of the white-tailed eagle he called the sea eagle, while to the adult form he gave the name white-tailed or cinereous.

In 1836 MacGillivary speaks of the sea eagle and the golden eagle being common in the Hebrides, but the golden eagle being more common in the Central Highlands.

A friend of mine has kindly copied from an old game book the record of vermin killed on the Glen Garry estate in 1839–40. There were accounted for (amongst less important "vermin") 27 sea eagles, 83 ring tails (immature golden eagles), 15 golden eagles.

Until about 1855 eagles bred in the lowland counties of Scotland (Dixon, *Lost and Vanishing Birds*).

In 1871 Yarrell (*British Birds*) mentions that the eagle is decreasing notwithstanding the protection afforded by some owners of deer forests. About the same date Gray mentions that the golden eagle is well known in all the Outer Hebrides.

There is now scarcely a single pair of eagles remaining in the Outer Isles.

In 1893 St John in his classic, *Wild Sport In the Highlands*, writes that the golden eagle was then still holding its own in the western districts of Scotland. It was preserved at that time by the Duke of Sutherland. It was still well known in the Outer Hebrides, especially Lewis and Harris.

The white-tailed eagle is spoken of as being common at this time too. It is also stated that there is a great demand for eggs by collectors and that a big price is paid for them.

In the *Vertebrate Fauna of Dee* (1903) it is mentioned that eagles have been "sorely reduced" owing to the war of extermination lasting fifty years.

In the late Osgood Mackenzie's *A Hundred Years in the Highlands* it is mentioned that ten eagles were killed two seasons

A YOUNG EAGLET AFTER AN EARLY FLIGHT.

running, and seven eagles two seasons running in his part of Ross-shire. This would be about 1906–10.

Eagles formerly bred in the more mountainous districts of England and Ireland as well as in Scotland. In Dumfriesshire they continued to nest until 1833, and in Kirkcudbright until about 1850.

It appears that the "balance of nature" was left undisturbed by man until about 1770 in Scotland, but even as early as the year 1330 there is an instance of bird protection, for what reason is not known, in Nichole Forest in Liddesdale on the Scottish border.

From about 1770 to 1860 a war of extermination was carried on against all birds of prey, during which time the goshawk and the kite were exterminated in the Highlands. Then protection of certain of the raptores began spasmodically, but it was too late to save the osprey and the sea eagle, the kite and the goshawk.

At the present day the golden eagle is in no danger of extinction. It is decreasing in the Central Highlands, but I think that this is owing to egg collectors rather than to game preservers. I am probably situated in a district that is unusually attractive to "eggers," because it is on the main line, and one can, if necessary, leave London in the evening, dine, sleep, and breakfast on the train, rob an eagle's eyrie during the day, return to London that evening and be back at one's office the following morning. Certainly in my particular district almost every eagle's eyrie is harried yearly, and as the eagle very rarely lays a second time if her first clutch be taken, it is not to be wondered at that the species is not so numerous as formerly.

Although the erne or sea eagle is probably lost to us as a nesting species, no book on the eagle would be complete without some account of the iolair bhuidhe (yellow eagle), as it was called by the Gael. How speedily a bird may become exterminated is evident from the following passage written by Gray in 1871 (*Birds of the West of Scotland*): "Being a much *commoner* bird in Scotland than the golden eagle, the sea eagle has never at any time been *in the same danger of extinction* (the italics are mine). In 1868, between Loch Brittle and Copnahow Head in Skye, for example, nine or ten eyries might have been seen. One of the most picturesque eyries of the erne on the west coast is, perhaps, that placed on the breast of one of MacLeod's Maidens (isolated rock stacks at the north entrance to Loch Bracadale). It also nested on Wiay."

But Gray elsewhere speaks prophetically of the extinction of the erne, for he writes: "It is impossible, however, to conceal the fact that if the present destruction of eagles continues we shall soon have to reckon this species among the extinct families of our feathered nobility. 'During the last nine years,' says my friend Dr Dewar, 'a keeper in Skye has shot fifty-seven eagles on a single estate.' Captain Cameron of Glen Brittle also informs me that he has now seen as many as sixty-two sea eagles killed in Skye. No species of eagle could long survive such persecution."

Henry Graham wrote from Iona to Gray as follows: "My friend Mr C. McVean has had a tamed sea eagle for some years which sometimes startles strangers by sweeping past the windows. He says: 'My eagle I named Roneval, after the hill in South Uist where he was hatched. I have had him now for four years, and he has assumed his white tail. He is allowed to fly about at large, but is not fond of going far, and will always come at the call of the kitchen-maid, who feeds him and for whom he shows the greatest affection. This personage, indeed, can manage him even when in most ungovernable tempers. He has a particular aversion for small boys, and will fly at one going near him. The only animal he is afraid of is a pig, and to hear a pig grunt is enough to make him fly off even if it should not be in sight. A well-dressed friend ventured one day to touch him with the point of his fashionable light umbrella, which so offended Roneval's majesty that he flew at the offending instrument and literally smashed it, breaking the stick and tearing the silk to tatters.

"Usually he is affable enough, and does no more mischief than occasionally killing a hen or two if his own dinner is not served up punctually enough; and this is really great forbearance, considering that he actually lives at large in a poultry yard. This proves how very domestic the monarch of the cliffs may become; for although a short-winged flight would carry him to the illimitable freedom of the neighbouring sea-cliffs and mountain-tops, he has never been known to 'stop out of nights' more than once or twice during a residence of several years."

The late Captain Allan Macdonald of Waternish had two tame sea eagles. They used to perch affectionately on the shoulders of the man who fed them, and were free to come and go as they pleased. When a rabbit was held out at arm's length, one of the eagles, which had been soaring in the clouds, at once stooped to the ground and snatched the rabbit without fear. The following two stories from the Outer Isles no doubt refer to the erne. A servant-girl of Sir Norman MacLeod of Bernera was tending cattle on the small isle of Hamarstray, in the Sound of Harris. She saw what seemed to be a *currach* or coracle with sail set coming before a smart breeze toward the isle.

When it reached the shore she discovered that the craft was the carcase of a cow and the sail the spread wings of an eagle. The talons were so firmly embedded in the cow that the bird was unable to escape. The girl unloosed the talons, and the eagle thereupon fixed them in her thigh, tearing out the flesh from the bone.

When the late Alexander Carmichael, author of *Carmina Gadelica*, was at Barra Head in June 1868 he was told of an eagle which carried away a lamb from Barra. The eagle was seen and pursued, but took to sea with its booty and disappeared. Two or three years later the owner of the lost lamb was driven by stress of weather into Tiree on passage to Greenock with a skiff full of fish, flesh, eggs, and fowls. The man in whose house he took shelter had a few sheep sharing the fire along with him, as was the custom in those days. The sheep were of a peculiar breed, and resembled those the storm-stayed visitor had at home. In course of conversation the Tiree man said that two or three years before, while he and his family were at the harvest near the shore one day they saw an eagle coming in from the sea with something white in its talons. It alighted exhausted on a knoll, and when they ran up it left a ewe lamb, badly torn but alive, on the ground.

The lamb was carefully tended and successfully reared, and in time had lambs of its own. The two men compared dates, and there seemed no doubt that the lamb was the one carried off from Barra. The distance between the two islands is about thirty miles.

The sea eagle did not nest on the coast only. For many years a pair nested on an island of Loch Baa, in the Blackmount Forest, and they are said to have nested as far from the sea as Braemar.

Wolley (*Ootheca Wolleyana, 1864*) mentions that he has seen two nests of different years on separate islands in one loch, each only about four feet above the ground, in very small trees. The same authority also writes: "When swimming is necessary it is often an affair of danger, as the birds will do their best to drown the enemy with their wings, but once he is out of the water they have the discretion to keep their distance.

"An eyrie in a small alder tree had been repaired and often frequented by the sea eagles the season I saw it, yet a hooded crow had eggs in the upper branches, and wild geese and ducks were sitting in the deep moss and long heather within twenty yards."

Wolley mentions heaps of herring-gulls' remains and the beaks of guillemots at a sea eagles eyrie, and writes that some of the eyries are made chiefly of seaweed. He also mentions that the erne is a week or a fortnight later than the golden eagle in laying.

Wolley, like Gray, realised that although the sea eagle was numerous when he wrote, it could scarcely stand the ruthless war of extermination waged against it. He states: " It is a melancholy reflection that the erne can scarcely exist much longer. The birds in their sea-girt fortresses will be the last to disappear, but each inland Creag an Iolair (Eagle's Rock) will soon be an empty name."

Wolley thus describes a Caithness eyrie: "On 21st April I visited the headland. On reaching the place and looking over, there was the bird on the nest, tail outwards and head under the ledge. The male was screaming to her from the rock below where we were standing. There were two eggs in the nest. The birds sailed with motionless wings in circles more and more distant; a screaming gull came to bully them, and looked very small in comparison.

"On Monday, 23rd April, having borrowed a coil of ropes from some fishermen, I drove over with a companion to the headland and put up at the lighthouse, where the keeper and two hands, an old sailor and a young labourer, were to meet me at the nest; a fourth man, a shepherd, also met me on the road to take the ropes and the bags. My companion agreed to make the necessary signs. I had a board to sit on, a tie round each thigh, and a piece under my arms.

"The nest was made of grass and fine fresh heather, very loosely put together – different from all the other nests I saw afterwards. Some pieces of guillemot, quite fresh, were lying about near the nest. The site was a considerable grassy ledge where grew statice, armeria, etc.

"The year before a very heavy thunder-shower happened just before my descent (to the same area), and a stream of water poured down almost into the nest, the greater part of which we arrested by canals cut in the turf with my knife. The young, fully fledged and grown, crouched with their heads towards the rock and allowed their legs to be tied without resistance. I fastened them with thick string to my rope, and their additional weight, with an occasional grip they gave the rock, made the pulling up very hard work for the men. In the nest were many bones of young herring-gulls and one of a large fish.... The feeling in an eagle's nest was sublime: the sea far below; the storm in the distance; the voices of men shouting, not to be understood; the expectation of a hostile visit from the old eagles; not to speak of the sensation that the rope might possibly be cut, a knot fail, the men faint, the post yield, a mass of rock fall down, and the like. The heather and peat might give way with the men, a flash of lightning terrify them."

To sum up. The erne, white-tailed eagle or sea eagle, has disappeared from Britain so far as is known, and yet sixty years ago it was apparently as numerous, if not more so, than the golden eagle.

The golden eagle in some districts is decreasing, in others holding its own, and in others perhaps showing a slight increase. Taking the Highlands of Scotland all over, it is probable that the golden eagle is holding its own, and it is to the credit of many landowners that they preserve it despite the grouse it takes.

Why, then, has the erne disappeared while the golden eagle continues to haunt hill and glen? In the first place, the erne preyed upon lambs more commonly than the golden eagle, so that the hand of every shepherd was against it. In the second place, its haunts were chiefly along the coast, where it could be easily kept under observation, while the golden eagle nests inland, in more remote places and mainly in deer forests. In the third place, the erne is much more of a wanderer than the golden eagle, and young sea eagles have time and again been shot along the east coast of England on their south migration.